Materials

os

Janet Taylor

Series editor: David Sang

CAMBRIDGE
UNIV

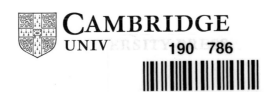

PUBLISHED BY THE PRESS SYNDICATE OF THE UNIVERSITY OF CAMBRIDGE
The Pitt Building, Trumpington Street, Cambridge, United Kingdom

CAMBRIDGE UNIVERSITY PRESS
The Edinburgh Building, Cambridge CB2 2RU, UK
40 West 20th Street, New York, NY 10011–4211, USA
477 Williamstown Road, Port Melbourne, VIC 3207, Australia
Ruiz de Alarcón 13, 28014 Madrid, Spain
Dock House, The Waterfront, Cape Town 8001, South Africa

http://www.cambridge.org

First published 2002

Printed in the United Kingdom at the University Press, Cambridge

Typeface Swift   *System* QuarkXPress®

A catalogue record for this book is available from the British Library

ISBN 0 521 79748 9 paperback

Produced by Gecko Ltd, Bicester, Oxon

Front cover photograph: Basalt columns, Ireland; Telegraph Colour Library

Contents

Introduction

Cambridge Advanced Sciences

The *Cambridge Advanced Sciences* series has been developed to meet the demands of all the new AS and A level science examinations. In particular, it has been endorsed by OCR as providing complete coverage of their specifications. The AS material is presented as a single text for each of biology, chemistry and physics. Material for the A2 year comprises six books in each subject: one of core material and one for each option. Some material has been drawn from the existing *Cambridge Modular Sciences* books; however, the majority is entirely new.

During the development of this series, the opportunity has been taken to improve the design, and a complete and thorough new writing and editing process has been applied. Much more material is now presented in colour. Although the existing *Cambridge Modular Sciences* texts do cover some of the new specifications, the *Cambridge Advanced Sciences* books cover every OCR learning objective in detail. They are the key to success in the new AS and A level examinations.

OCR is one of the three unitary awarding bodies offering the full range of academic and vocational qualifications in the UK. For full details of the new specifications, please contact OCR:

OCR, 1 Hills Rd, Cambridge CB1 2EU

Tel: 01223 553311   http://www.ocr.org.uk

The presentation of units

You will find that the books in this series use a bracketed convention in the presentation of units within tables and on graph axes. For example, ionisation energies of $1000\,\text{kJ}\,\text{mol}^{-1}$ and $2000\,\text{kJ}\,\text{mol}^{-1}$ will be represented in this way:

Measurement	Ionisation energy ($\text{kJ}\,\text{mol}^{-1}$)
1	1000
2	2000

OCR examination papers use the solidus as a convention, thus:

Measurement	Ionisation energy / $\text{kJ}\,\text{mol}^{-1}$
1	1000
2	2000

Any numbers appearing in brackets with the units, for example $(10^{-5}\,\text{mol}\,\text{dm}^{-3}\,\text{s}^{-1})$, should be treated in exactly the same way as when preceded by the solidus, $/10^{-5}\,\text{mol}\,\text{dm}^{-3}\,\text{s}^{-1}$.

Materials – an A2 option text

Materials is all that is needed to cover the A2 physics option module of the same name. It is a brand new text which has been written specifically with the new OCR specification in mind. At the end of the book you will find a glossary of terms and answers to self-assessment questions.

This module is intended to build upon the AS and A2 core material covered in *Physics 1* and *Physics 2*. It is advised that these titles are studied before this *Materials* module.

Acknowledgements

Photographs

P.2a,b, 1.18, Claire Davis, University of Birmingham; P.2d,e, Dr Mark Aindow; 1.1, © The Natural History Museum, London; 1.4, Monsanto; 1.16, © Michal Heron/Woodfin Camp Associates; 1.19b, Corus; 1.24 a,b,c,d,e, Neil Thompson; 1.37, 1.39, 3.2, 3.18, Dr James Marrow, Manchester Materials Science Centre, UMIST and University of Manchester; 1.43, Prof. M. J. Whelan, Philosophical Magazine 1956; 2.14a, 2.27b, Andrew Lambert; 2.16b, Associated Press; 2.21, P. P. Edwards, Dept. of Chemistry, University of Birmingham; 2.22, R. K. Papworth, Cavendish Laboratory, University of Cambridge; 2.23, © Milepost 92½; 2.24, David Scharf/Science Photo Library; 2.26, courtesy of Unilab; 3.8, 3.9, American Institute of Physics; 3.12b, Janet Taylor; 4.12, Standard Telecommunication Laboratories; 4.13, Darwin Dale/Science Photo Library; 4.15, © Guzelian/Professor C. J. Humphreys

Diagrams

Cambridge University Press would like to acknowledge the following publishers whose diagrams appear in this book: 1.5, Tomorrow's Materials, Ken Easterling, Maney Publishing/Institute of Materials, 1.7, 1.17, 1.34, Teacher's Pack on Experiments in Materials Science, Claire Davis, Maney Publishing Institute of Materials; 1.9, 1.13, Patterns in Physics, W. Bolton, Nelson Thornes (McGraw-Hill UK); 1.10, 1.11, 1.14, 1.19a, 1.37a, 1.44, 2.5, 2.6, 4.5, 4.6, 4.13, Materials Science and Engineering, Willian D. Callister, John Wiley & Sons, Inc.; 1.20, 2.7, 2.8, 3.7, 3.17, Materials in Action, Materials, Principles and Practice, Eds Newey and Weaver, Butterworth-Heinemann/Open University; 1.22, 1.41, Engineering Materials 1, Ashby & Jones, Pergamon Press; 1.38, OU Foundation, Living With Technology T101, The Open University; 2.14, RS Data Sheet 232–3816 (CD-ROM), The Open University; 2.19, Reactions and Characteristics of Solids, Sandra Dann, Royal Society of Chemistry; 3.11, Rose, Shepard & Wulff, John Wiley & Sons, Inc.; 3.14, Introduction to Materials Science and Engineering, Ralls, Coutney & Wulff, John Wiley & Sons, Inc.; 4.14, Wilson & Hawkes, Prentice Hall

Prelude

Why 'Materials'?

The *Materials* in the title of this book refers to the discipline of materials, an advanced area of science which brings together physicists, chemists and engineers. The materials you will meet here are in the solid state. They are generally made and used for practical purposes, such as carrying mechanical loads, conducting electricity or transmitting light.

If you have followed a GCSE Science course, you may have come to associate the study of materials with chemical science. In that context all forms of matter, in whatever state, were thought of as 'materials'. This book treats materials from the angle of physics and engineering. It is divided into four chapters, each focussed on a group of physical properties. The aim is to show how the behaviour of solids depends on their atomic, molecular and crystalline structure and, at the same time, to provide further insights into the mechanical, electrical, magnetic and optical properties of materials. The relevance of many of these properties to industry and society gives the book a technological flavour.

Classifying materials

The modern approach to studying materials starts from the arrangement of the atoms. In this book materials are described as crystalline, polycrystalline, amorphous and semi-crystalline. However it is useful to be aware of the traditional classification in which materials are divided into four classes; metals, polymers, ceramics and glasses, and composites. Composites are made from mixtures of the materials in the first three classes. The relationships are summarised in

figure P.1. The scheme is based largely on the chemical make-up of the materials and the type of bonding between the atoms, topics which are outside the scope of the current book. (*Table 1.1* on page 7 offers a brief summary of the origin and types of bonds).

As scientists understand more fully how properties depend on underlying structure it has become possible to design or engineer a material with a particular property or combination of properties. Researchers have also synthesized new materials, such as high-temperature superconductors, with exceptional or even completely novel properties.

Looking at materials

In the following pages you will find images of materials at different magnifications. The theme of the book is the relationship between the *macro*scopic behaviour of a material and its

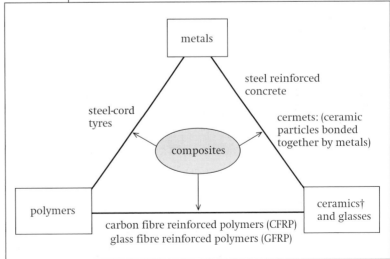

● **Figure P.1** The traditional classification of engineering materials. Examples of composites, materials which consist of more than one of the other three classes, are given.
†Ceramics are inorganic compounds of metallic and non-metallic elements. They are often oxides, nitrides or carbides and include porcelain, concrete and cement. They are typically more resistant to high temperatures than metals or polymers. Mechanically they are very hard but brittle.

Size of structural feature	Type of microscope used
micrometres (μm) to millimetres (mm) 10^{-6} m to 10^{-3} m	Light – optical
0.02 micrometres (μm) to millimetres (mm) 2×10^{-8} m to 10^{-3} m	Scanning electron microscope (SEM)
nanometres (nm) to micrometres (μm) 10^{-9} m to 10^{-6} m	Transmission electron microscope (TEM) Scanning-transmission electron microscope (STEM)
single atoms (approx. 10^{-10} m)	Atomic force microscope (AFM) Scanning tunnelling microscope (STM)

● **Table P.1** Microscopes used for examining the microstructures of materials.

*micro*structure. 'Macroscopic' describes behaviour on the scale at which we see and use objects in daily life. A microstructure is, in contrast, 'visible under a microscope'. Since this term was first used, new techniques have lowered the limit on the size a microscope can resolve. The scanning tunnelling microscope (STM) and atomic force microscope (AFM) can display images of atoms. Because magnifications can range up and down through many powers of ten, it is essential to note the scale when you examine an image. *Table P.1* summarises the dimensions of the microstructures made visible by the different techniques. *Figure P.2* shows examples of the images obtained.

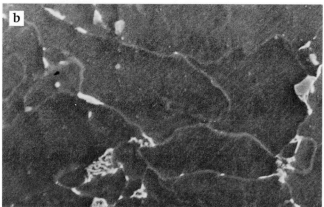

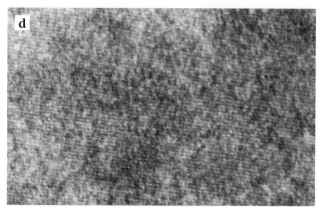

● **Figure P.2** Photographs of a type of steel using different techniques: **(a)** optical microscopy (× 100); **(b)** scanning electron microscopy (× 300); **(c)** transmission electron microscopy (× 1300); **(d)** high resolution electron microscopy (× 50 000); **(e)** computer visualisation from atomic force microscope (× 400 000).

Mechanical properties and microstructures

Classification of solids

Solid materials can be classified in several ways. In this book you will find that in many cases they are described as being either **crystalline** or **amorphous**. For our purpose, which is to explore how physical properties are determined by the behaviour of atoms and electrons, the question of whether or not a material is crystalline often turns out to be significant. In a crystal the atoms are arranged in orderly repeating patterns. Here, and in the following chapters, you will see how the presence or absence of these patterns, and the arrangement and spacing of the atoms, influences the properties of materials. A description of

crystalline and amorphous microstructures is therefore a good place to begin.

Polycrystalline solids

Almost all metal and ceramic objects are in fact **polycrystalline**. They are, as the term implies, made up of many crystals. When you look at a metal object, say a spanner, this is not evident, although there are rare instances where the crystalline character of metals is more obvious. The piece of mined copper shown in *figure 1.1* is an example. Here you can see the flat surfaces and symmetrical shapes of the crystals. You will know

● **Figure 1.1** A sample of mined copper. The planes on the surfaces of the crystals can be seen.

single crystal (*Physics 2*, Chapter 12). The interlocking crystals are called **grains** and the very thin surfaces which separate them are called **grain boundaries**. At a grain boundary the repeating patterns of the crystal do not line up. This is illustrated in *figure 1.2*, which is a two-dimensional representation of interlocking crystals.

Later in this chapter you will see how grains can be made visible under a microscope. They are an important part of the microstructure because they influence mechanical and other properties.

that these features reflect the orderly arrangement of atoms inside the material. However, crystalline solids do not necessarily show outward signs of the order within. A solid is defined as crystalline when its atoms are stacked in a regularly repeating three-dimensional pattern. The pattern repeats over extended regions so that in any direction there are thousands of atoms in an orderly array.

Inside a polycrystalline solid the crystals interlock to form a solid mass. Although they do not have regular shapes, X-ray, neutron and electron diffraction techniques can be used to reveal the regular repeating patterns of the atoms in each

Single crystal solids

A diamond gem stone is an example of a single crystal solid. The regular array of atoms (*figure 1.3*) extends right through the stone. There are some applications where it is necessary to have a

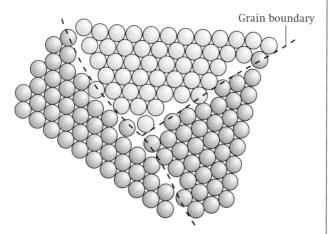

● **Figure 1.2** A two-dimensional diagram representing a polycrystalline solid. The crystals are called 'grains' and are separated by grain boundaries. Each grain has the same regular repeating pattern, but the pattern does not line up across the grain boundaries.

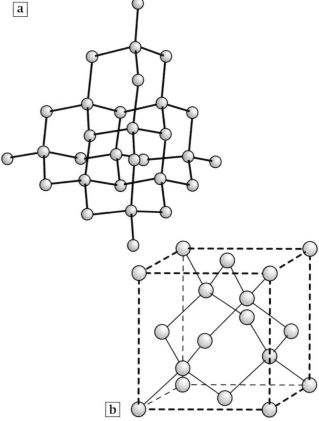

● **Figure 1.3** The crystal structure of diamond. **a** Each carbon atom is bonded to four other carbon atoms. **b** The repeating unit in the crystal structure.

Box 1.1 Single crystal silicon for the electronics industry

The silicon used in semiconductors is exceptionally pure, with less than one impurity atom per 10^9 atoms of silicon. The crystals are grown by dipping a small 'seed' crystal held on the end of a long rod, into a crucible of molten silicon. By slowly withdrawing and rotating the rod a crystal up to a metre long is pulled and grown (*figure 1.4*). The cylindrical crystals are called ingots. The ingots are sliced into wafers about 0.725 mm thick and with a diameter of 30 cm. Each wafer is then polished until it has a mirror-smooth surface. It will provide a base on which integrated circuits are fabricated. These are three-dimensional many-layered structures, the layers having different electrical properties. Some layers are added while in others the silicon is 'doped' by injecting small quantities of atoms from different elements (see page 35). Imperfections in the crystal structure and the presence of grain boundaries would interfere with these processes.

- **Figure 1.4** A single crystal or ingot of silicon is pulled and grown. It is then sliced into wafers for the manufacture of integrated circuits (chips).

material in the form of a large single crystal. The silicon used to make integrated circuits (chips), such as those at the heart of computers, is an example. The silicon, which has a similar crystal structure to that of diamond, is grown as a single crystal, or ingot (*box 1.1*). The crystals are then sliced into 'wafers', providing thin pieces of perfect silicon on which integrated circuits can be built. The structure and composition of the layers has to be controlled at the level of the atoms. The single crystal is therefore grown under very carefully controlled conditions.

molecular order but the regular repeating pattern does not extend into space as it does in the crystal. The structure of the glass is disordered whereas the crystal has symmetry.

The glass structure looks rather like a still image of a liquid. It is not a liquid because it cannot flow (the characteristic property of a liquid). Instead, each atom occupies a fixed position within the structure (strictly speaking this is a mean position about which the atom vibrates). In principle, all crystalline materials can also exist in an amorphous state if the molten material is cooled quickly enough. Very rapid cooling, by

Amorphous solids

The atoms in an amorphous solid occupy random positions. *Figure 1.5* shows the arrangement of silicon and oxygen atoms in silica **glass** (*a*) compared with that in a silica crystal (*b*). The three-dimensional network in the glass is a distorted version of that in the crystal. The molecular structure of the glass, which is the same as that of the crystal, imposes some short-range

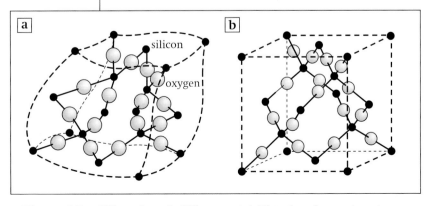

- **Figure 1.5 a** Silica glass. **b** Silica crystal. The glass has a structure like a randomly distorted version of the crystal.

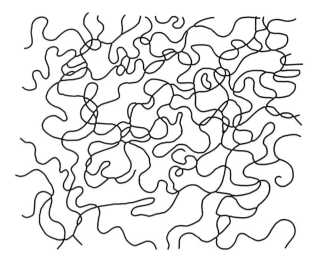

● **Figure 1.6** The randomly coiled chains in an amorphous polymer. In a glassy polymer the chains are fixed in position and cannot flow past each other.

about a million degrees per second, can effectively 'freeze' the random arrangement of atoms in a liquid metal. Amorphous metals are very uncommon, but they do exist and have specialised applications on account of their unusual magnetic properties (chapter 3).

Some polymeric materials are described as '**glassy polymers**' because they share some of the properties of glass. They have replaced glass in many traditional applications such as transparent roofing, spectacle lenses and bottles for fizzy drinks. Like glass they are brittle although they do not break into dangerously sharp fragments (giving them an advantage in most applications). Glassy polymers have an amorphous structure. As you will already know, polymers are made up of many thousands of units (monomers) linked together in long chains. They very often have a 'backbone' of carbon atoms. In an amorphous polymer the chains

are randomly coiled (*figure 1.6*). The solid is rigid because the chains cannot rotate and slide past each other.

SAQ 1.1
a Polymers have replaced glass in many applications. Give an example where a polymer is superior to glass. Identify the properties which make the polymer a better choice.
b Glass is better than plastic for some applications. Suggest two properties where glass has the advantage.

Semi-crystalline polymers

Polymers differ widely in their mechanical properties. They behave as they do because of the way their long chains are arranged. The glassy polymers we have just met are amorphous. Polymers such as polyethylene nylon and PVC (polyvinyl chloride) contain both amorphous and crystalline regions. They are described as **semi-crystalline** and are flexible and **tough**.

In the crystalline regions the chains line up with each other. One way for this to happen is by a long chain folding back on itself. You can see this in *figure 1.7a* which shows the structure of polyethene (polythene). *Figure 1.7b* shows the regular

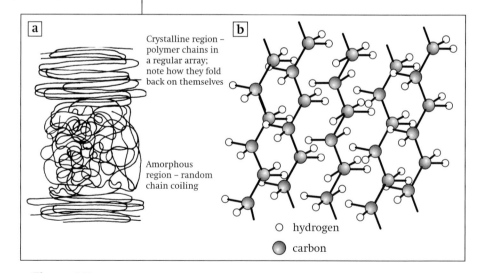

● **Figure 1.7**
a The structure of polyethene. The polymer chains in the crystalline region fold back on themselves in a regular array. In the amorphous regions the chains bend and coil in a disordered, random structure.
b The regular arrangement of the carbon and hydrogen atoms in the crystalline region.

arrangement of the carbon and hydrogen atoms in the crystalline regions. They are held together by weak instantaneous dipole-induced dipole (Van der Waals') forces (see *table 1.1*). The presence of the crystalline regions gives the material stiffness.

The chains in the amorphous regions bend and coil at random. Although glassy polymers are rigid at normal temperatures they tend to soften when they are heated. Perspex (polymethyl methacrylate) is an example. There is a landmark temperature (known as the glass transition temperature) which marks the change in properties. Above this temperature the long chains are no longer fixed in position. They are able to bend and twist and move past each other so that the material can be deformed. In a semi-crystalline polymer the transition temperature is well below room temperature. As a result the amorphous regions are soft, giving the material flexibility.

You may have seen some of these effects if you have investigated polymers (*Physics 1*, chapter 8). They can be explained in terms of the degree of crystallinity and the effects of temperature. The details are beyond the scope of this book, and we will now return to crystalline solids.

SAQ 1.2
What techniques have you met which give you evidence about the arrangement and spacings of the atoms in a solid? You may like to look back at *Physics 2* to answer this.

Crystal structures
To understand relationships between structures and properties we need to take a closer look at crystals. In a crystal a regular arrangement of

Type of bond	Bond Strength	Class of material	Examples	Bonding mechanism	Crystalline structure
Ionic	Strong	Ceramics	Sodium chloride	Atoms lose and gain electrons to form ions. The crystal is an array of ions in which opposite charges attract and like charges repel. The net effect is an attraction between neighbouring ions	The crystal is an array of ions. Because the field round a charge extends in all directions, one ion attracts several ions of opposite charge. The ions pack closely together to give electrical neutrality
Covalent	Strong	Ceramics In polymers the units of the long chains are linked by covalent bonds	Diamond Silicon	Electrons are shared between neighbouring atoms	Giant molecules with bonds in definite directions. The packing is determined by the valency and valency directions
Metallic	Strong	Metals	Potassium Copper	Positive metal ions surrounded by a 'sea' of electrons	Forces between ions and electrons are not in definite directions and favour close-packing
Instantaneous dipole-induced dipole forces (Van der Waals')	Weak (Van der Waals' bonds exist between all atoms and molecules)	Polymers Large biological molecules e.g. proteins and nucleic acids	Solid methane Crystalline regions of polymers	Electron clouds are polarised. Attractive forces arise between negative regions on one atom and positive regions on another	Weakly attracting units are close-packed. Bonds are not directional
Hydrogen bonding	Weak	Large biological molecules e.g. proteins and nucleic acids	Hydrogen bonds connect H_2O molecules in ice crystals	The nucleus of a bound hydrogen atom (a proton) is attracted to the electrons on a neighbouring atom	The bond is directional and determines the packing

● **Table 1.1** The main types of bonding in solids.

atoms extends over distances which are very large compared with the diameters of the atoms. Every atom occupies a point in space on a three dimensional **lattice**. The pattern is formed by the regular repetition of groups of atoms, the term **unit cell** being used to describe the smallest repeating unit. Crystals hold together because there are bonds between atoms. You may like to glance at *table 1.1* to remind yourself of the different types of bond.

If the atoms in a solid behaved like hard spheres you might expect them to fit together in the most compact arrangement possible. This is what happens in many metals. A metal lattice is formed by positive ions held together by a 'sea' of electrons. The bonds are not directional so that metals prefer lattice arrangements where the atoms can fit snugly together surrounded by other atoms. In other materials the bonding may dictate that the atoms are more spaced out. In diamond and silicon, for instance, each atom has only four 'nearest neighbours' in a tetrahedral array (*figures 1.3* and *2.10a*).

Most metals have crystal structures of one of three types. Two are **close-packed** and are described below. The third type, body-centred cubic, is not close-packed. It is described briefly in *box 1.2* on page 10. It occurs in iron and is important for the formation of steels. You will see later that the crystal structure of a metal can influence its mechanical properties.

Close-packed crystal structures

Close-packing

Here we imagine the atoms (or ions) as hard spheres and pack them together as closely as possible. You may find it helpful to build some of the structures for yourself. This can be done using 5 cm polystyrene spheres or table tennis balls and a flat box. First fit as many identical spheres as you can into a single layer and you will see that they arrange themselves so that each sphere is surrounded by six others (*figure 1.8*).

Then, if a second layer is packed on top of the first it will sit in the depressions between the spheres in the first layer. In *figure 1.9*, A is the first layer and B is the second layer. When a third layer is added there are two possibilities. The first (*figure*

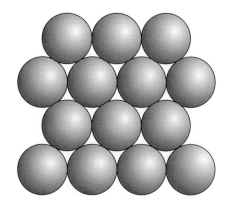

● **Figure 1.8** Spheres arranged in a close-packed layer.

1.9a) gives hexagonal close-packing while the second (*figure 1.9b*) gives cubic close-packing.

Hexagonal close-packing

In hexagonal close-packing the spheres in the third layer fit into the depressions lying directly above the spheres in layer A. This makes it the

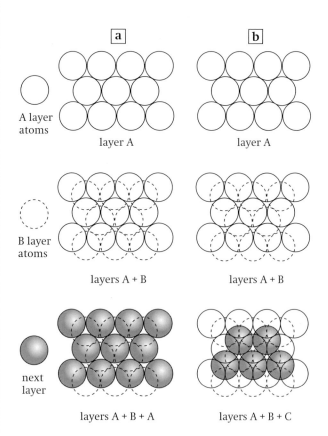

● **Figure 1.9** Different ways of stacking close-packed layers of spheres.
a Layer sequence ABABAB... giving hexagonal close-packing.
b Layer sequence ABCABCABC... giving cubic close-packing.

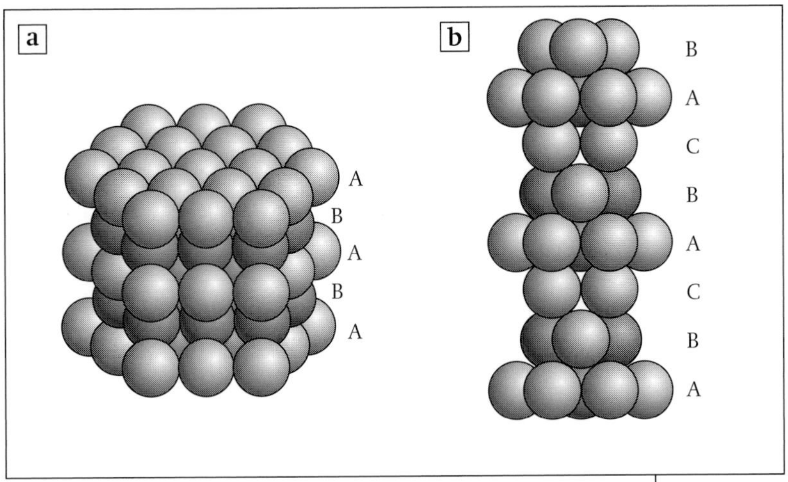

• **Figure 1.10**
a Stacking in a hexagonal close-packed crystal structure.
b Stacking in a cubic close-packed crystal structure.

same as layer A so that the pattern is described as ABABAB. *Figure 1.10a* shows the sequence in 3-dimensions. The crystal structure is called **hexagonal close-packed** (h.c.p.). The **unit cell** (*figure 1.11*) has hexagonal symmetry. In this structure each atom is surrounded by 12 'nearest neighbours'. Magnesium, cadmium, zinc, titanium and nickel are among the common metals that have this type of structure.

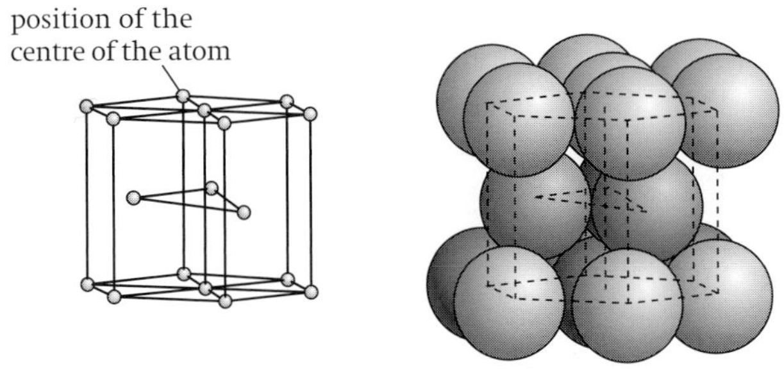

• **Figure 1.11** The unit cell in a hexagonal close-packed structure. On the left, the small circles show the positions of the centres of the atoms.

Face-centred cubic

The alternative form of close-packing is shown in *figures 1.9b*, *1.10b* and *1.12*. Here a third layer is placed on top of B but each sphere now fits in a depression lying above a space in layer A. The third layer is called C because it is displaced relative to A and B. The stacking sequence is ABCABCABC. In this structure each atom is again surrounded by 12 'nearest neighbours'. The unit cell is a face-centred cube (*figure 1.12*) and the arrangement is described as 'cubic close packing'. The cubes are difficult to visualise unless you actually build the structure and stick the spheres together. If you do not have a three-dimensional model you may find the diagram in *figure 1.13* helpful. It shows the relationship of the unit cell to the close-packed planes. Aluminium, lead, copper, gold, silver, gold and platinum have this type of crystal structure, which is known as **face-centred cubic** (f.c.c.).

Why does copper have a face-centred cubic structure and zinc a hexagonal close-packed structure? The answer is that the f.c.c. structure gives copper the least energy and the h.c.p. structure gives zinc the least energy.

Within both h.c.p. and f.c.c. crystals there are certain planes in which the atoms are close-packed, in the pattern shown in *figure 1.8*. Close-packed planes can also act as 'slip planes', a term which describes their role in the way materials deform. You will meet it later, in the explanation of plastic deformation on page 21.

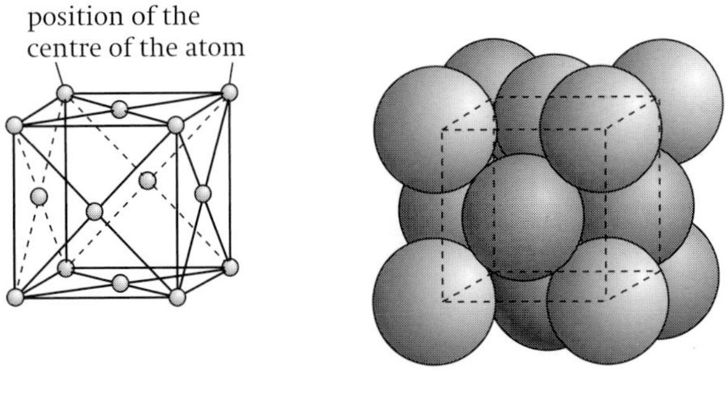

• **Figure 1.12** The face centred cubic (f.c.c.) unit cell.

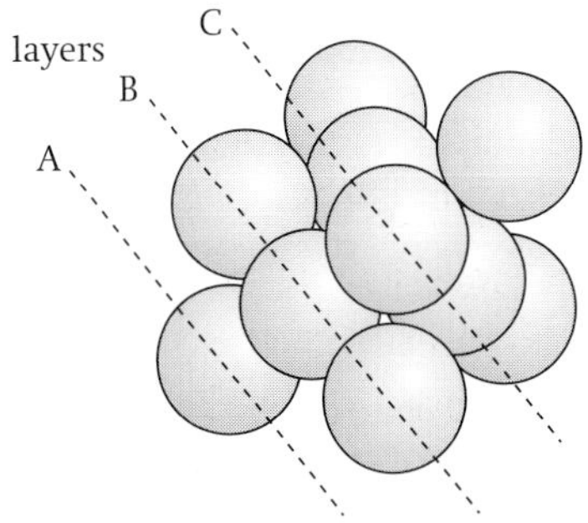

• **Figure 1.13** The relationship of the face centred cubic unit cell to the stacked layers (A,B and C) of cubic close-packed spheres.

It is straightforward to identify the close-packed planes in an h.c.p. crystal. They lie parallel to the base of the unit cell (*figure 1.11*) and are the A and B planes from which we built the crystal. There are no other close-packed planes in this type of structure.

In contrast to this, f.c.c. crystals have close-packed planes in four directions. The A, B and C planes in *figure 1.9b* are, of course, close-packed. To

find the others you need to imagine a cubic crystal, made up from many unit cells (*figure 1.14*). 'Slicing off' one corner diagonally exposes a close-packed plane of spheres. Since this can happen at each corner of the cube there are four 'families' of parallel close-packed planes within the crystal. If you look back at the raw copper crystals in *figure 1.1*, you can recognise sloping faces corresponding to these close-packed planes.

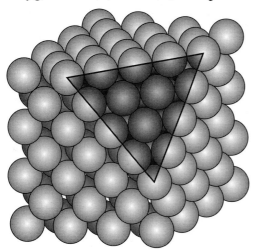

- **Figure 1.14** A face-centred cubic crystal. Notice that the planes on the sides of the cube are not close-packed. 'Slicing off' the corners reveals the close-packed planes; they lie in four directions, corresponding to the corners of the cube.

- **Figure 1.16** The stacks of oranges and apples in this photograph form flat sloping faces. They illustrate the way metal atoms form crystals.

Box 1.2 Body-centred cubic crystal structure

In general a material assumes the crystal structure having the lowest energy and this is not necessarily close-packed. In the case of metals, about 20% have a crystal structure known as body-centred cubic (b.c.c.). At room temperatures iron has this type of crystal structure. The unit cell is shown in *figure 1.15*. There is an atom at each of the eight corners of a cube and another atom in the centre. You can see that each atom in this structure has eight nearest neighbours. From its appearance you might think that the b.c.c structure is just as compact as h.c.p. and f.c.c. but calculations show that this is not the case. Potassium, chromium, molybdenum and tungsten have b.c.c. crystal structures.

Many elements have different structures at different temperatures. This is known as 'polymorphism'. It happens because the minimum energy crystal structure at one temperature is not the same as that for another temperature. The most important metal to show this effect is iron. At room temperature the crystal structure of iron is b.c.c. (α-iron) but it changes to f.c.c. (β-iron) on heating to 910 °C.

The alloys or mixtures formed when carbon is added to iron are the basis of the many types of steel. In simple or plain carbon steel the carbon atoms sit in the holes in between the iron atoms in the b.c.c. or f.c.c. structures. The

transformation from b.c.c. to f.c.c. is very important in the heat treatment of steels.

SAQ 1.3

Iron changes from b.c.c. to f.c.c. at 914 °C. A sample of iron is heated. What happens to the volume when it reaches this temperature?

position of the centre of an atom

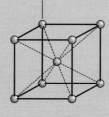 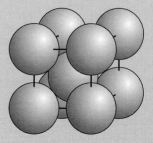

- **Figure 1.15** The body centred cubic (b.c.c.) unit cell.

SAQ 1.4
Displays of oranges and apples are often stacked to show smoothly sloping faces of close-packed fruit (*figure 1.16*). Identify some of the close-packed planes in the photograph. The packing corresponds to one of the crystal structures you have just met. Which is it?

Grains and grain boundaries

A polycrystalline material is a solid mass of single crystals. In *figure 1.17* you can see how crystals form when metal solidifies. Bonds form at the boundaries where the crystals meet, but the regularly repeating pattern of atoms is interrupted. The arrangement of the interlocking single crystals is known as the 'grain structure'.

Grain sizes vary from 10 μm to several millimetres. It is sometimes possible to see the larger size with your unaided eye (*figure 1.18*), but they are generally too small.

Grains can be made visible under a microscope. *Box 1.3*, overleaf, explains how this is done.

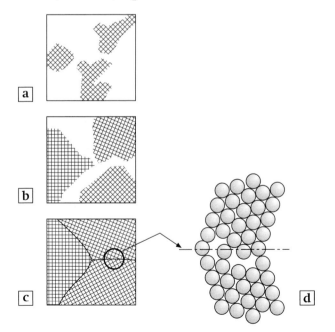

● **Figure 1.17** As the molten metal cools tiny crystals appear at centres of nucleation in the liquid (**a**) and begin to grow (**b**). In many metals the crystals take the form of dendrites, spiky solids which branch at right angles. When the dendrites meet, (**c**), the last of the liquid solidifies between the branches. Each dendrite becomes a single crystal or 'grain' separated by a grain boundary (**d**).

● **Figure 1.18** Photograph of a galvanised lamp post showing grain structure.

The size, shape and orientation of the grains in a polycrystalline solid influences its properties. The grain structure can be controlled and modified during the manufacturing processes that shape a material into a finished product (e.g. rods, tubes, car body panels, turbine blades, transformer cores etc.). These processes include extrusion, injection moulding, casting, forming and heat treatments. In practice the microstructure of a solid is inseparable from the object that it forms. We do not, however, deal with manufacturing processes in this book.

Imperfections in crystals

Even in the most perfect crystals a few atoms are not in exactly the right position in the lattice. We say that the lattice contains imperfections or defects. You might well suppose that their presence would affect its properties only slightly. In fact, defects do have great significance, because they govern important mechanical (and other) behaviour. For instance, they cause the stress at the elastic limit to be very much smaller than that predicted for a perfect lattice – as much as 10^5 times smaller in some metals.

Point defects

As the name suggests, a point **defect** is linked with a single site in the lattice. The simplest kind is a **vacancy**. This is an empty lattice site which would normally be occupied by an atom. In the

Box 1.3 Looking at grains under a microscope.

The metal is cut into pieces and the cut surface of a sample is polished and then etched. The atoms in the grain boundaries are more chemically active than the others so that they tend to dissolve at a greater rate, forming grooves. The boundaries then show up under the microscope because the grooves reflect light at an angle different from the grains themselves (*figure 1.19*).

The surfaces of the grains can also vary in appearance. The crystal planes in the grains are, as we have seen, at varying angles to the surface. The etching fluid can preferentially attack certain planes, making one grain reflect light differently from another (*figure 1.20*). *Figure 3.18* on page 54 was obtained in this way. It shows the silicon steel used in transformer coils.

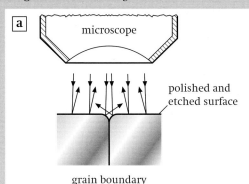

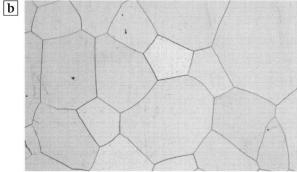

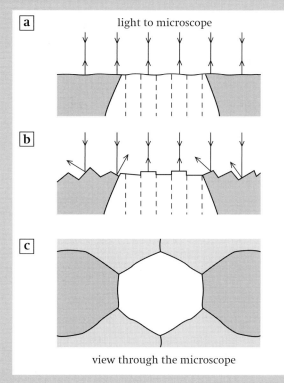

- **Figure 1.19** Examining grain structure using a microscope.
a Diagram showing a cross section though a sample of metal which has been polished and etched. Light hitting the groove is not reflected back into the microscope.
b Photomicrograph of a polished and etched polycrystalline specimen of an iron-chromium alloy in which the grain boundaries appear dark. The magnification is ×100.

- **Figure 1.20** A schematic diagram showing how etching can make grains appear differently under a microscope.
a Before etching the incident and reflected rays coincide. The dotted lines represent planes in the crystal.
b After the surface has been etched, some grains reflect light back through the microscope while others do not.
c The grains now appear light, grey and dark.

region around it the lattice tends to become distorted (*figure 1.21a*).

A point defect also occurs when an impurity atom replaces one of the atoms in the lattice. If it is different in size to the lattice atoms it can create strains in the lattice. It is called a substitution defect. (*Figure 1.21b*). A third type of point defect arises when an impurity atom squeezes itself into a space in the lattice. This is called an interstitial defect. It can also be a source of strain (*figure 1.21c*).

Dislocations

A **dislocation** is a defect which exerts a profound effect on the mechanical properties of a material. You will see later in this chapter how the presence of dislocations allows materials to deform plastically (permanently) at low stress levels. The dislocation arises because there is an extra half-plane of atoms in the lattice. It is shown in three dimensions in *figure 1.22*. Dislocations were put forward as a hypothetical mechanism for plastic deformation long before they were observed.

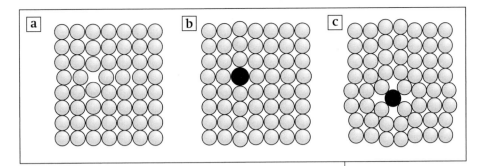

● **Figure 1.21** Point defects.
a A vacancy can appear in the lattice.
b An impurity atom has substituted one of the
  atoms in the lattice.
c An impurity atom has fitted into a space in the
  lattice.

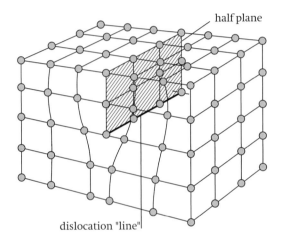

● **Figure 1.22** A dislocation, shown for simplicity in
a cubic framework.

Making models in two-dimensions

Try using ball-bearings or a bubble-raft to model
grain boundaries and crystal defects in two-
dimensions.

■ **Ball-bearing models**
Ball-bearings in a petridish will produce a two-
dimensional close-packed hexagonal array. You
may be able to obtain a simple piece of
equipment built expressly for this purpose. It
consists of a single layer of ball-bearings sand-
wiched between transparent glass or plastic
plates. Placed on top of an overhead projector
it makes an effective demonstration. The ball-
bearings are free to move and, when gently
shaken, settle into patterns like that shown in
figure 1.23. Here you can see both grain boundaries and vacancies. A plane which contains a

dislocation is indicated but
the extra half plane of atoms
is not obvious. You will find a
bubble raft superior for
demonstrating dislocations.

■ **Bubble raft**
The bubbles are formed on
the surface of a flat rectangular dish which, as for the
ball-bearing model may be positioned on an
overhead projector (figure 1.24a). The aim is to
form a raft of bubbles about 10 cm × 10 cm. Two
barriers laid across the surface of the trough
allow the bubble raft to be stretched and
compressed between them. The barriers can be
wooden batons or pieces of wire.
A suitable solution can be made by mixing one
part washing-up liquid with 32 parts of water.
Eight parts of glycerol may be added to make
the bubbles last longer. Bubbles can be blown
using the gas supply, an air pump or a large
air-filled syringe. They should be formed slowly
(a few a second) and they should be small
(1–2 mm diameter).

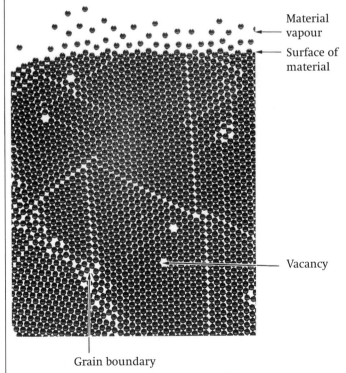

● **Figure 1.23** Ball-bearing model showing how
atoms pack together in solids. The model shows
the grain boundaries in a polycrystalline material
and vacancies caused by missing atoms. The model
also shows another type of defect, the dislocation.

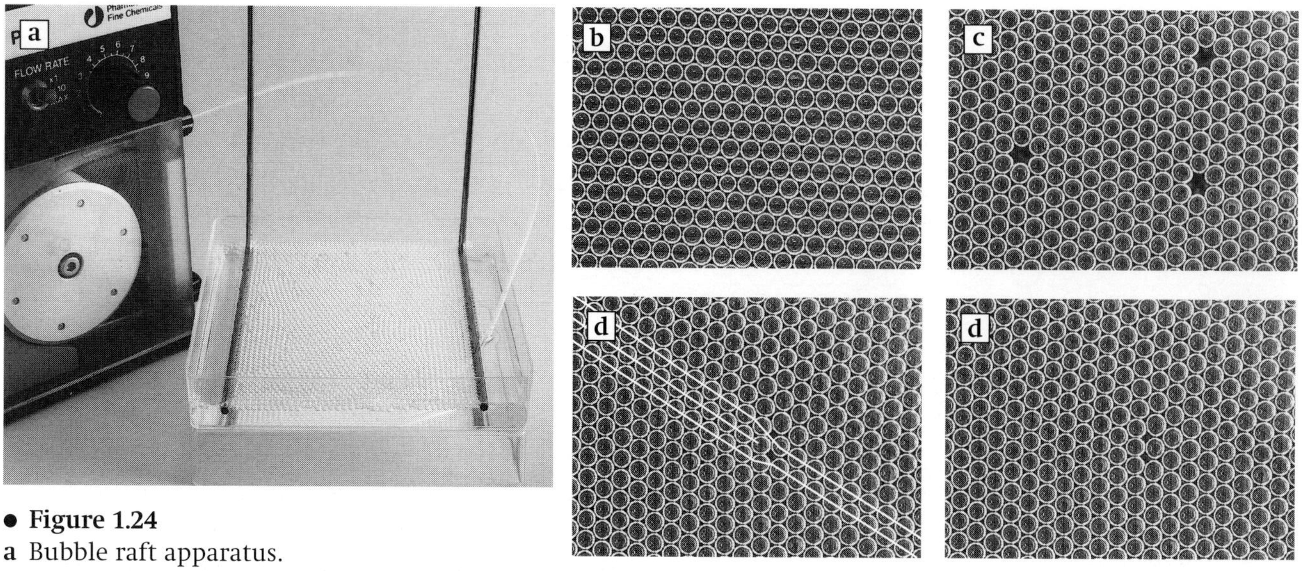

● **Figure 1.24**
a Bubble raft apparatus.
b A regular close-packed array of bubbles. The arrows correspond to crystal planes in a three-dimensional solid which act as slip planes.
c A vacancy (one type of point defect).
d A dislocation. The two photographs are the same but lines have been drawn on one to show the dislocation. Note that you could draw the lines from top right to bottom left and still show the dislocation.

Large areas of the raft will show a regular close-packed hexagonal array (*figure 1.24b*). You should see grain boundaries where two differently oriented regions meet. A vacancy (*figure 1.24c*) can be made by popping an individual bubble using a *dry* needle. Another type of point defect can be demonstrated if a bubble of larger size is introduced. Around it you will see that the lattice is slightly distorted. A dislocation is shown in *figure 1.24d*. Dislocations are less easy to spot but can be detected if you move the barriers to compress and stretch the raft; they become more visible as they move through the lattice. When you have found one, try making it move backwards and forwards. Notice that it gets absorbed when it reaches a grain boundary. Both the ball-bearings and the bubble raft are two dimensional. The rows of atoms represent planes in a three-dimensional crystal. The arrows in *figure 1.24b* correspond to the planes which act as 'slip planes'. You can read about their significance on page 21.

How solids behave under mechanical stress

'.... and only think that all those structures you have about you – think of the 'Great Eastern', if you please, which is of such size and power as to be almost more than man can manage – are the result of cohesion and attraction.'
Michael Faraday (1791–1867), On the various forces of Nature.

In its day the Great Eastern, at 211 m and 32 200 tons, was the largest steamship in the world. It was designed by Isambard Kingdom Brunel and launched in 1858. Engineers continue to take structures to their limits with longer bridges, taller buildings and faster aeroplanes. It is still a matter of wonder that such awesome structures ultimately depend on the forces of attraction and repulsion between individual atoms.

Before we begin to explore the connection between macroscopic properties and interatomic forces you may like to look back at *Physics 1*, Chapter 8 'Deforming Solids' to remind yourself how mechanical properties are measured. There you saw that many solid materials deform in an elastic manner until the stress reaches a value known as the *elastic limit*. Behaving elastically means that they return to their original shape when the stress is removed. If the atoms have fixed positions in a lattice it is clear that the dimensions of the lattice will change when the solid is deformed. If the solid is stretched the separation between individual atoms will increase in the direction of stretching. On compression the atoms will be squashed together so that the separation will decrease. If the solid is elastic there must be restoring forces to bring the atoms back to their original positions. To see how these forces arise we now set up a model of how the forces between atoms and molecules vary with their separation.

The forces between atoms and molecules

Forces of attraction

The attractive forces that hold solid materials together arise from bonds. The different types were summarised, with examples, in *table 1.1*. You are not expected to recall the bonding mechanisms but should note that metallic, ionic and covalent bonds give strong attractive forces while van der Waals' forces and hydrogen bonds are weak.

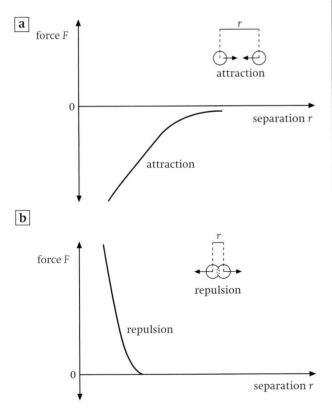

● **Figure 1.25** Curves showing how **a** the attractive force and **b** the repulsive force might vary with the separation between two atoms or molecules.

In every solid the force of attraction increases as the atoms or molecules approach. The graph in *figure 1.25a* shows how it might vary with the separation between a pair of particles. At large separations the force declines to zero, as you would expect. You will see notice that the *attractive* force is taken to be *negative*. (This follows a convention according to which a force in the opposite direction to r is negative; you may find other books treat 'attraction' as positive.)

Forces of repulsion

If the only forces between atoms were attractive then matter would collapse inwards. It is clear that there must be repulsive forces. They arise because, when atoms are brought very close together, the electron clouds around neighbouring atoms begin to overlap. Like charges repel each other so the electron cloud around one atom repels that around its neighbour. The closer the atoms and their charge clouds approach the stronger the force becomes.

When we packed atoms together (page 8) we imagined them to be hard spheres. In fact the repulsion between the electron clouds keeps the atomic centres a fixed distance apart. At this separation, which is called the **equilibrium separation** (r_0), the repulsive force exactly balances the attractive force.

It is evident, from the way solids resist compressive forces, that the atoms cannot be pushed much closer together. This tells us that the force of repulsion rises steeply when r decreases from r_0. A curve showing how the repulsive force varies with separation is sketched in *figure 1.25b*. According to our sign convention a repulsive force, which acts in the same direction as r, is positive.

The force–separation curve

The attractive force can be combined with the repulsive force to give the net or **resultant force** between the particles for each value of the separation. Since force is a vector the directions of the forces must be taken into account. According to our convention attraction is negative and repulsion is positive. Summed in this way the curves in *figure 1.25* give the solid curve in *figure 1.26*. This curve shows how the resultant force varies with separation. Although, as you would expect, the

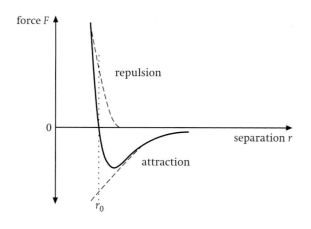

● **Figure 1.26** The solid curve shows the variation with separation of the resultant force between a pair of atoms. It is the vector sum of the attractive and repulsive components (broken lines). The equilibrium separation is r_0.

Box 1.4 Constructing a force–separation curve

Figure 1.27 shows how the attractive component (F_A) and the repulsive component (F_R) of the force between a pair of atoms might vary with their separation (r). To construct the force–separation curve you may like to make a copy so that you can plot the points directly on the page. Otherwise a simple table can be made with column headings as shown.

r (10^{-10} m)	F_A (10^{-9} N)	F_R (10^{-9} N)	$F_A + F_R$ (10^{-9} N)

Choose a value of the separation and read off the corresponding values for F_A and F_R from the curves. Enter them in the table. Find the sum of F_A and F_R and enter it in the last column. (If you have a copy of the graph you can plot the point immediately.)

Repeat this procedure for a range of values between 2.88×10^{-10} m and 3.60×10^{-10} m. *Table 1.2* shows a typical set of readings.

You can now take the values of $F_A + F_R$ from the table and plot them against the separation of the atoms (*figure 1.28*). You should be able to recognise the general features that have been described.

r (10^{-10} m)	F_A (10^{-9} N)	F_R (10^{-9} N)	$F_A + F_R$ (10^{-9} N)
2.88	−5.25	6.8	1.55
3.00	−4.0	4.0	0.0
3.12	−3.0	2.4	−0.6
3.24	−2.2	1.4	−0.8
3.36	−1.6	0.8	−0.8
3.48	−1.2	0.55	−0.65
3.60	−0.8	0.4	−0.4

● **Table 1.2**

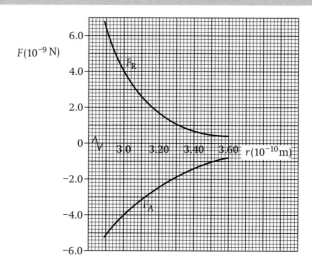

● **Figure 1.27** Graph showing how the attractive component, F_A, and the repulsive force, F_R, between a pair of atoms might vary with their separation.

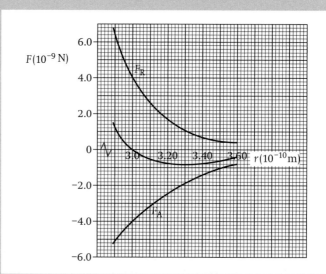

● **Figure 1.28** The resultant force–separation curve calculated as the vector sum of attractive and repulsive components.

curve varies from one material to another, it always fits the following description.

The value of r where the curve cuts the axis gives r_0, the equilibrium separation, since the sum of the components at this point is zero. Below r_0 the force is a repulsion which increases very rapidly as r decreases. Above r_0 the resultant force is attractive. As the separation increases beyond r_0 the attractive force gets larger but eventually reaches a point when it begins to fall. The highest value of the attractive force corresponds to the minimum on the graph. After this the force gradually approaches zero. You will see later that the curve can be linked to properties of materials that can be measured. It is a good idea to practise sketching it so that you can recall its general shape.

You may find it useful to work through the quantitative example in *box 1.4*. Here the scales on the axes gives values for the attractive and repulsive forces at different separations for a particular material.

SAQ 1.5

What value does the force–separation curve in *figure 1.28* predict for the equilibrium separation of the atoms?

Explaining elastic behaviour

Materials which recover after a deforming force is removed are described as *elastic*. The force–separation curve that we have just described can explain elastic behaviour in many types of solid.

When there is no external force acting on the material the distance between the atoms will be r_0, the equilibrium separation. What happens when a material is deformed? If the material is under compression the separation between neighbouring atoms may become less than r_0. If this happens then the net force between the atoms is a repulsion. It will push the atoms back to their original positions when the compressing force is removed. If the material is stretched, so that r becomes greater than r_0, the net force between the atoms will be attractive. When the stretching force is removed this attractive force comes in to play, bringing the atoms back to their original positions.

You may like to note that rubbers, which behave reversibly at very high strains, owe their elasticity to another mechanism which we do not cover in this book. The configuration of the molecular chains in stretched and unstretched rubber is shown in *figure 1.29*.

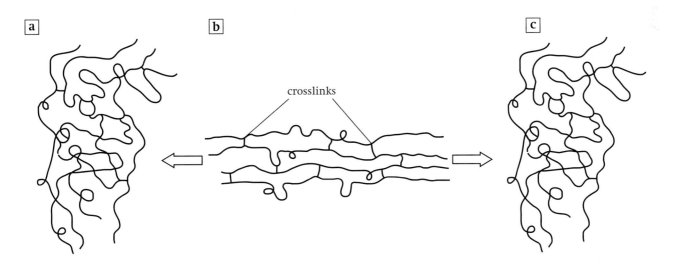

● **Figure 1.29**
a The molecular chains in unstretched rubber are highly coiled, twisted and kinked.
b Under a tensile stress (see force arrows) the chains partially uncoil, untwist and straighten out. As a result the sample gets longer in the direction of the stress.
c When the stress is removed the chains go back to their prestressed conformations. This is because the molecules prefer to be in the more disordered state. The explanation lies in thermodynamics and is outside the scope of this book.

Hooke's law

Hooke's law says that, when an object is stretched or compressed, the change in length in the direction of the tensile (stretching) or compressing force is proportional to the force. A graph showing change in length against applied force will be a straight line. You saw in *Physics 1* chapter 8 that springs behave like this and learnt that many solid materials obey Hooke's law. The shape of the force-separation curve explains why.

SAQ 1.6

(revision) Write definitions for the terms **stress** and **strain**.
What units are used for stress?
Strain has no units. How is it often expressed?

If you look back at the stress-strain graphs for metals and glass in *Physics 1* you will see that the strains which occur below the elastic limit are less than 0.1%. We therefore need to look at the way the resultant force varies with the separation at values of r only very slightly below and above r_0.

In *figure 1.30* this region of the curve has been magnified. For values of r very close to r_0 it gives a

straight line graph. We can write the equation for the line as

$$F = k\Delta r$$

where Δr represents a very small change in r. The interatomic forces are making the atoms behave as though they are linked by a spring which obeys Hooke's law. k, the gradient of the force-separation curve at the equilibrium separation, is the 'spring constant' of the atomic spring. The sign convention we have adopted, according to which an attractive force is negative, makes k appear negative on the graph.

Using force-separation graphs to estimate the Young modulus

We can now relate the shape of the force-separation curve to the **Young modulus**. You will

Material	Young modulus E $(10^9 \, \text{N m}^{-2})$
Diamond (natural)	700–1200
Silicon carbide	207–483
Tungsten	406
Chromium	289
Nickel	214
Iron	196
Stainless steel	190–200
Platinum	172
Copper	124
Titanium	116
Copper alloys	97–150
Silicon	107
Silica glass, SiO_2	94
Aluminium	69
Silver	76
Soda glass	69
Ice	9.1
Nylon 6,6	2–4
Polystyrene	3–3.24
Polyethene	0.2–0.7
Foamed polymers	0.001–0.01

Many of these values depend on the processes used in manufacturing the material and on its precise composition.

● **Table 1.3** Data for the Young modulus E.

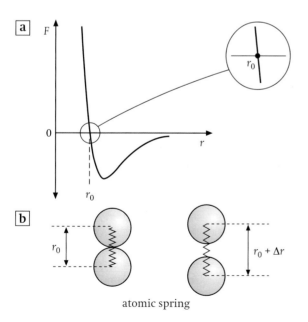

● **Figure 1.30**
a The force-separation curve. The inset shows, enlarged, the region around r_0. Here the graph approximates to a straight line.
b An 'atomic spring' extends by Δr when it is stretched.

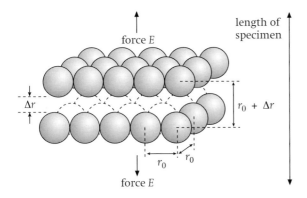

- **Figure 1.31** A crystalline solid in which the atoms are in a simple cubic array. Stretching (by means of forces F) increases the separation between every pair of planes by Δr.

recall from *Physics 1* that the Young modulus is the property of a bulk material which measures stiffness. It is the ratio of stress to strain when deformation is elastic and is given the symbol E. Values for the Young modulus of various materials are given in *table 1.3*.

To estimate a value of E from the force-separation curve we imagine that the pairs of atoms are in a crystal lattice. To simplify the calculation we make the lattice cubic. In *figure 1.31* you can see two planes of atoms. They are perpendicular to the length of the specimen. The crystal is being stretched so that the planes have become separated by a distance Δr. Every pair of planes in the crystal will be separated by the same amount. Each bond acts like a tiny spring.

We will use A to represent the cross-sectional area of the specimen. Because the lattice is cubic the total number of atoms that can be fitted into the cross-sectional area will be A/r_0^2. If the force exerted by a single atomic spring is F, the total force between the planes will be F multiplied by this number or

$$\frac{AF}{r_0^2}$$

Hooke's law for the spring tells us that $F = k\Delta r$ so that the force between the planes is

$$\frac{Ak\Delta r}{r_0^2}$$

The Young modulus, E, for the material is the ratio $\dfrac{\text{stress}}{\text{strain}}$.

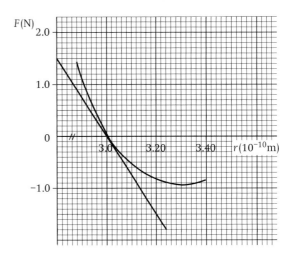

- **Figure 1.32** A tangent is drawn to the force-separation curve in order to calculate k.

In this case stress = $\dfrac{\text{force between crystal planes}}{\text{cross-sectional area}}$

i.e. $\dfrac{\text{total force}}{A}$

$$= \frac{Ak\Delta r}{r_0^2 A} = \frac{k\Delta r}{r_0^2}$$

The strain is $\dfrac{\Delta r}{r_0}$

So, the Young modulus, $E = \dfrac{\text{stress}}{\text{strain}} = \dfrac{k\Delta r r_0}{r_0^2 \Delta r} = \dfrac{k}{r_0}$

This means that we can read k and r_0 from the force-separation curve and then calculate E. In *figure 1.32* the curve in *figure 1.28* has been redrawn. To find k a tangent is drawn to the curve at the equilibrium separation. The gradient of the tangent is about $-6.1 \times 10\,\text{Nm}^{-1}$. The equilibrium separation is $3.0 \times 10^{-10}\,\text{m}$. Using these values in the equation above, and allowing for the sign convention, we obtain

$$E = \frac{k}{r_0} = \frac{6.1 \times 10}{3.0 \times 10^{-10}}\,\text{Nm}^{-2} \quad \text{or} \quad 2.0 \times 10^{11}\,\text{Nm}^{-2}.$$

This is within the range of values for the Young modulus found for metals.

SAQ 1.7

The force separation curves for two materials A and B are shown in *figure 1.33*. Which of these materials will have the higher value of the Young modulus?

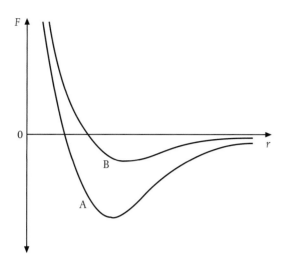

● **Figure 1.33** Force separation curves for two materials, one weakly bonded and the other strongly bonded.

Breaking stress

Another striking feature of the force-separation graph is the minimum corresponding to the highest value of the resultant force when attractive. How can we interpret this? Would a simple calculation based on this value give the force needed to break a crystalline solid apart? The calculation goes like this.

We take the highest value of the resultant force between two atoms, in the part of the curve where this force is attractive, and call it F_{max}. Following the reasoning in the previous section, the total force across a plane is FA/r_0^2 and the corresponding stress in the crystal will be F_{max}/r_0^2. According to our simple model this is the stress at which the material breaks.

The quantitative curve in *figure 1.32* can be used to test this idea. It gives a value for F_{max} of 9×10^{-10} N. Since r_0 is 3.0×10^{-10} m, F_{max}/r_0^2 is 10^{10} Nm^{-2} i.e $10\,000$ MNm^{-2}. *Table 1.4* shows the **ultimate tensile strengths** of various metals for comparison. The treatment above predicts a much higher value of the breaking stress than is actually found in tensile tests on real metals.

The value of the separation of the atoms at the minimum on the curve in *figure 1.32* casts further doubt on the interpretation. In this example it is 3.3×10^{-10} m, which would correspond to a strain ($\Delta r/r_0$) of 10%. We have already noted (page 14) that almost all materials show some permanent deformation when the strain is greater 0.1%. The crystal planes, shown in *figure 1.31*, do not pull further and further away from each other; something else happens. When a metal is stretched beyond its elastic limit (which is lower than the ultimate tensile stress) **plastic deformation** sets in. The crystal planes begin to slide over each other causing permanent deformation. (The mechanism will be explained in more detail in the next section.) You will have seen how a copper wire gets thinner ('necks') before it breaks. As it narrows the

---

Box 1.5 Brittle fracture

Ceramics, glassy materials and a few metals break by a mechanism called brittle fracture.

The diagram (*figure 1.34a*) shows a tiny narrow crack producing a high local stress at its tip. The top rod has no surface flaws and the stress at all points in the rod is the same. The lower rod has a narrow crack. The stress becomes concentrated at the tip of the crack. The presence of a sharp crack only 2×10^{-6} m deep can magnify the stress 100 times. The local stress at the crack tip is large enough to break apart the interatomic bonds. The crack then spreads between a pair of atomic planes as the bonds break in rapid succession. This does not occur in a ductile material because in them planes of atoms can slide past each other, causing the crack to become blunted.

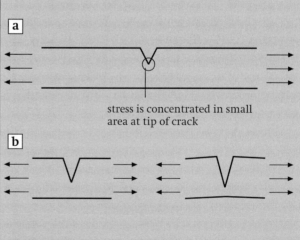

● **Figure 1.34**
a A surface crack causes stress to concentrate at its tip.
b The stress causes the bonds to break, so that the crack grows.

Material	Ultimate tensile strength (MN m^{-2})
Tungsten	1510
Steels	380–1760
Nickel	400
Iron	200
Copper	400
Aluminium	200

Many of these values depend on the processes used in manufacturing the material and on its precise composition.

● **Table 1.4**

cross-sectional area of the sample is reduced so that the true stress becomes larger. Internal cavities (or other flaws) then develop in the wire and reduce the effective cross-sectional area still further (*figure 1.35*). Finally the stress becomes high enough to tear the atoms apart.

Ceramics also break in tensile tests at much lower applied forces than predicted. This can be explained by very small structural flaws which act as 'stress-raisers'. They amplify the effect of the tensile stress and initiate cracks, which lead to fracture. This is explained further in *box 1.5*.

Plastic deformation and slip planes

When a metal deforms plastically the atomic planes slide past each other (*figure 1.36*). Depending on the material, the slip occurs on a particular crystallographic plane, which is usually the plane of closest-packing. This is the reason why the close-packed planes in the crystal structures we have met are called **slip planes**.

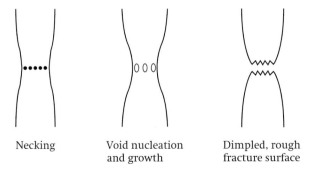

Necking   Void nucleation   Dimpled, rough
           and growth   fracture surface

● **Figure 1.35** Schematic diagram showing how internal cavities develop in a wire during a tensile test. **a** The wire 'necks'; **b** voids nucleate and grow; **c** the wire fractures leaving a dimpled rough surface.

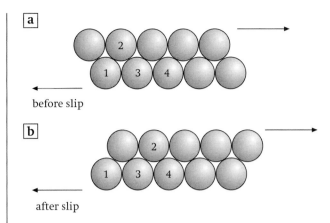

before slip

after slip

● **Figure 1.36** The planes of atoms within a grain slide past each other. The planes along which slip occurs are called slip planes.

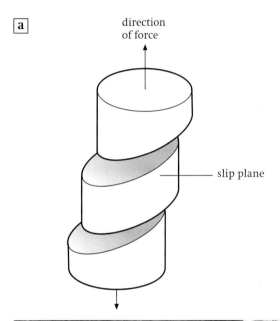

direction of force

slip plane

● **Figure 1.37**
a Slip in a single crystal.
b A single crystal of cadmium after it has been stretched along its length, × 60.

If a single crystal is stretched the slip will happen along planes which are favourably oriented to the direction of the tensile force (*figure 1.37a*). Slip produces lines on the surface of a polished single crystal specimen. You can see them in the photograph of a single cadmium crystal (*figure 1.37b*).

Figure 1.38 will remind you of a typical stress-strain graph for a ductile metal. Here the sample is a single crystal and the schematic illustrations show what is happening along the curve.

We have seen that slip, in a single crystal, occurs along a particular set of crystallographic planes. Earlier in this chapter we saw that f.c.c. crystals have four families of close-packed planes whereas h.c.p crystals have only one. It is therefore more probable that a single f.c.c. crystal will have a plane which is favourably oriented to allow slip. This explains why metals with an f.c.c. crystal structure tend to be more ductile than those with an h.c.p. structure. Single crystals of h.c.p. metals fracture rather than deform plastically, if their close-packed planes are not in a favourable orientation for slip to occur.

Deformation in a polycrystalline material is more complex because such a material cannot behave like a single crystal. Slip does occur but in

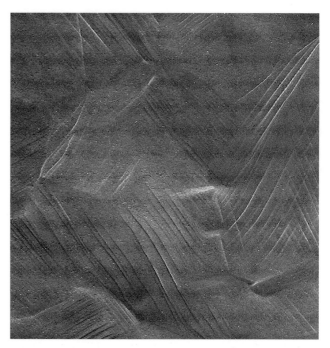

● **Figure 1.39** Slip lines on the surface of a polycrystalline specimen of copper, × 2500.

ways that allow the grains to remain in contact. *Figure 1.39* is a photomicrograph of a polycrystalline copper specimen that has been plastically deformed. Slip lines are visible and you can see that two families of slip planes are operating for most grains.

SAQ 1.8

Copper has a close-packed crystal structure. Which type does the photomicrograph in *figure 1.37* suggest it has? Explain your reasoning.

Dislocations and slip

When one plane slips over another each atom has to move from its original position to a site one atomic spacing away. The atoms do not move simultaneously. If we set up a theoretical model based on the assumption that they do, it fails to predict the low values of stress that cause plastic deformation in metals. Look at *figure 1.40*. If the atoms move in unison the planes have to separate slightly as the atoms pass over each other. It is possible to calculate the force needed to make this happen and use it to predict the stress at the elastic limit. This force turns out to be very much larger (by a factor of 10^5 in some metals) than the observed value.

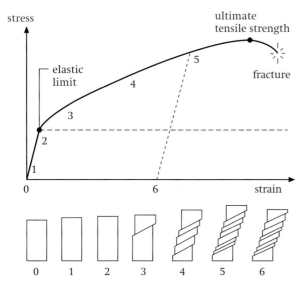

● **Figure 1.38** The stress-strain curve for a single metal. The schematic diagrams show slip producing plastic deformation at various points along the curve. Slip begins to occur at the elastic limit. At (6) the stress has been removed but the sample is permanently deformed.

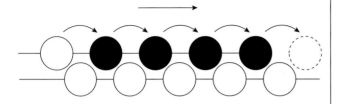

● **Figure 1.40** The model used to predict the stress required to produce simultaneous slip. This model turns out to be **incorrect**.

The mistake in the model is the assumption that the atoms move at the same time. The low value of the elastic limit can be explained if they move one by one. The presence of dislocations allows this to happen. You met this type of crystal defect earlier in this chapter. Look back at *figure 1.22*, which shows a dislocation in three dimensions. The concept of a dislocation was put forward to explain how slip occurs in 1934. This was twenty years before it was actually seen in an electron microscope image.

The diagrams in *figure 1.41* explain the slip mechanism. You can see how the bonds break and reform to allow a dislocation to move in *figure 1.41a*. *Figure 1.41b* shows a complete sequence as a dislocation moves from one side of the lattice to

the other. In a metal the bonds break and reform easily because they are not strongly directional. Ceramic crystals also contain dislocations but the bonds are directional so that the dislocations are less mobile. As a consequence ceramics do not deform by this mechanism.

The way a dislocation works is sometimes compared with the easy method of moving a carpet. It is hard to drag a heavy carpet by pulling the edge (*figure 1.42a*) but easy to put a wrinkle in the carpet and push it from one edge to the other (*figure 1.42b*).

In his book *The New Science of Strong Materials*, James Gordon tells how physicists used dislocations to solve problems long before there was compelling visual evidence that they existed (*box 1.6*). This evidence appeared in 1956 when moving dislocations were unexpectedly observed with the transmission electron microscope (*figure 1.43*). Heat from the electron beam itself expanded the sample, setting up stresses which made the dislocations move. Until then it was thought that thin dark lines seen in micrographs might represent dislocations (through an effect of lattice strain on the electron beam) but this was by no means certain. Now the lines were seen to dash about in astonishing confirmation that they were indeed dislocations.

Dislocations always glide along crystallographic planes. In a polycrystalline solid a dislocation cannot cross a grain boundary. You may have seen this effect in a bubble-raft model. In real materials the stress at which the metal or alloy deforms permanently can be increased if a metal or alloy has been processed so that the grains are of a small size. (We mentioned on page 11 that grain structure can be controlled and modified to produce useful properties.) Dislocations are very

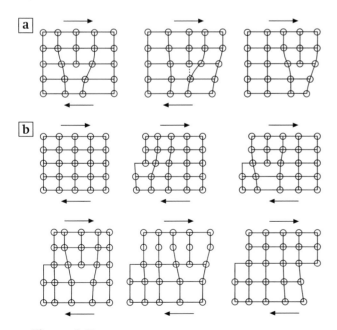

● **Figure 1.41**
a The atomic bonds break and reform to allow the dislocation to move.
b These six pictures show a dislocation moving right across the lattice. The planes slip by a distance equivalent to one atomic spacing.

● **Figure 1.42** The carpet wrinkle analogy of a moving dislocation.

Box 1.6 A working hypothesis

.........For many years nobody saw a dislocation in the flesh, or perhaps even expected to, but their hypothetical movements (dislocations of like sign repel each other etc.) and breeding habits (when the union of two dislocations is blessed about five hundred new dislocations are suddenly released upon the crystal) could be theoretically predicted and provided a superb intellectual exercise like three-dimensional chess. As a matter of fact nearly all these academic predictions turn out to be true. (Geoffrey Taylor) supposed originally that slip in ductile crystals was due entirely to those dislocations which were present initially in the crystal due to imperfect growth. It turns out that there are generally not enough dislocations originally present in most crystals to account for the very extensive slip which can take place in a ductile material. Large families of new dislocations can however be nucleated either by dislocation interaction or more frequently by severe stress concentrations, such as occur at crack tips. These mechanisms enable a stressed metal to be rapidly filled with dislocations and thus to flow under a steady load or blow of a hammer quite easily.

J.E. Gordon, The New Science of Strong Materials.

important in that they allow a process known as work-hardening (*box 1.7*). Metals are worked when they are rolled or drawn into wires. At the same time they become stronger. This is an example of a manufacturing process (see page 11) where the microstructure is modified to produce useful properties.

SAQ 1.9

When a single dislocation moves across a crystal the planes of atoms slide across each other by one atomic spacing. Estimate how many dislocations will be needed to produce a permanent extension of 1 mm.

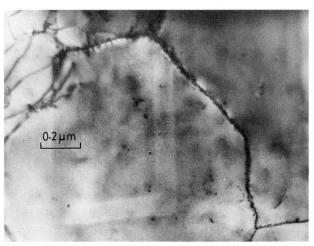

0·2 μm

Box 1.7 Work-hardening

Work-hardening is a very common method of improving the strength of metals. It also explains part of the shape of stress-strain curves in ductile materials. If the planes just continued to slip once the elastic limit was reached, the stress-strain curve would be a horizontal line past this point. In fact it still rises (*figure 1.44*).

As the strain goes up the stress needed to cause further strain gets higher. This means that the elastic limit increases as plastic deformation proceeds. There is no change in the Young modulus. The effect is due to dislocations, which multiply as the strain increases. They interact with each other and become locked in place in a 'traffic jam'. As the dislocations become less mobile it becomes more difficult to make the material deform permanently and the elastic limit increases.

Too much work-hardening can raise the elastic limit so much that the material becomes brittle. A heat treatment, called annealing, removes the effect. In this process the object is heated to a temperature which is below the melting point of the material but high enough for the atomic vibrations to release the dislocations. They free themselves and move to the edges of the grains, where new grain boundaries form. Dislocations also affect magnetic properties. You will see in chapter 3 that these processes are used when the microstructure of silicon steel is tailored for use in transformer cores.

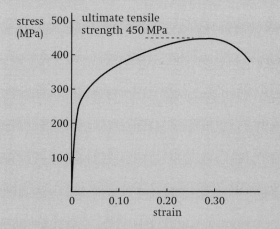

● **Figure 1.44** Typical stress-strain curve for a specimen of brass.

● **Figure 1.43** A transmission electron micrograph taken in 1956 by M.J.Whelan. The lighter strip with a right angle bend is the trace left by the movement of a dislocation through a sample of aluminium foil. It corresponds to the intersection of a slip plane with the surfaces of the foil. The rapid movement of the dislocation across the plane leaves a light trace that will later fade. The contrast is produced because when the electron beam is at a particular angle to the crystal planes the extent to which electrons are deflected is sensitive to tiny changes in the orientation of the planes.

SUMMARY

♦ The atoms in a crystalline material are in a regular, repeating, three-dimensional array. The pattern extends over many thousands of atoms. The structure has long range order.

♦ Amorphous materials are non-crystalline. The atoms or molecules are not arranged in a regular repeating pattern.

♦ Many polymers contain both crystalline and amorphous regions.

♦ Single crystal materials are materials in which the atomic order extends uninterrupted through the entire specimen.

♦ Most crystalline solids are polycrystalline. They are made of many small crystals, or grains, with different crystallographic orientations.

♦ If atoms are assumed to be hard spheres and if they are packed together as closely as possible the arrangement of the atoms is described as close-packed.

♦ There are two close-packed crystal structures:
  • In hexagonal close-packed (h.c.p.) structures the close-packed planes are arranged in successive layers ABABABAB...
  • In face-centred cubic (f.c.c.) structures the close-packed planes are arranged in successive layers ABCABCABC...

♦ A point defect is associated with a single point on the lattice.

♦ A dislocation is a linear defect in the crystal structure. It arises because there is an extra half-plane in the crystal lattice.

♦ Bubble-rafts and ball-bearing models can be used to illustrate point defects, dislocations and grain boundaries. They also illustrate 'slip planes', the planes of atoms along which slip takes place when a material undergoes plastic deformation.

♦ Elastic deformation occurs when an external force causes the distance between the atoms in the crystal lattice to increase or decrease reversibly. Interatomic forces restore the atoms to their original positions when the external force is removed.

♦ The forces of attraction and repulsion between two atoms each vary with the separation of the atoms.

♦ The resultant force between the two atoms is the vector sum of the forces of attraction and repulsion.

♦ The force-separation graph explains elastic behaviour and why crystals obey Hooke's law for small stresses.

♦ The force-separation graph does not predict the stress at which solids break or fail.

♦ At the equilibrium separation of two atoms the attractive force balances the repulsive force. On the force-separation curve the separation at which the resultant force is zero is the equilibrium separation.

♦ In plastic deformation slip occurs so that planes of atoms become displaced relative to each other. The 'slip planes' are the crystallographic planes along which slip occurs. In close-packed crystal structures these are the planes of closest packing.

♦ If all atoms in the planes were to move simultaneously, the force required to cause slip would be very much higher than that observed. Dislocations allow slip to occur at stresses corresponding to the elastic limit. Dislocations glide along crystallographic planes.

Questions

1 With reference to the arrangement of the atoms, distinguish between the structures of crystalline and amorphous solids.

2 a Draw diagrams to illustrate the arrangement of the atoms in the following close-packed structures:
  (i) hexagonal close-packed;
  (ii) face-centred cubic.
  b When a hexagonal close-packed structure is formed, the close packed planes are arranged in successive layers in a pattern. After how many layers does the pattern repeat?

3 Explain the terms **grain** and **grain boundary**. Use a labelled sketch of a two-dimensional model to illustrate your answer.

4 Sketch a graph to show how the resultant force F between two atoms varies with the separation r between their centres.
   Mark the **equilibrium separation** r_0 of the atoms on your graph. Indicate, on your graph, the regions where the resultant force between the two atoms is attractive and the regions where it is repulsive.

5 The graph in *figure 1.45* shows how the resultant force, F, between a pair of atoms in a crystal varies with their separation r.

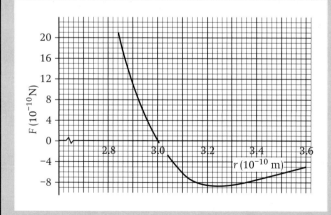

● Figure 1.45

a With reference to the graph, state the value of r at the equilibrium separation.
b The model represented by the graph can be used to explain the elastic behaviour of solids. Use it to explain:
  (i) why solids resist being stretched or compressed;
  (ii) why Hooke's law is obeyed for small changes in length of a solid rod.
c It can be shown that the **Young modulus** for a solid is approximately given by $E = k/r_0$ for small displacements, where r_0 is the equilibrium spacing between the atoms and k is the force per unit displacement between the atoms. Use the graph to make an estimate of k. Calculate the Young modulus, for the solid represented by the graph.

6 *Figure 1.46* shows the arrangement of the atoms in a crystal in the region of a dislocation.

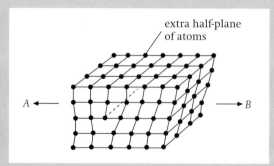

● Figure 1.46

Using labelled diagrams, show how the dislocation moves when stress is applied in directions A and B.

Explain why the stress required to deform a perfect crystal is greater than that required to deform one containing dislocations.

CHAPTER 2

Electrical properties of materials

By the end of this chapter you should be able to:

1 define *electrical conductivity* as the reciprocal of electrical resistivity;

2 distinguish between the *r.m.s. speed* and the *drift velocity* of an electron which forms part of an electric current in a solid;

3 derive and use $I = nAve$ for a single charge carrier in a solid;

4 appreciate that in a solid material the outer electrons of neighbouring atoms interact;

5 distinguish between the *conduction band* and the *valence band*;

6 use *band theory* to describe the conduction of electrons in metals;

7 recall that there is an *energy gap* between the conduction band and the valence band and that an electron cannot have a value of energy corresponding to the range of values defined by this gap;

8 use band theory to explain qualitatively the electrical properties of metals, insulators and intrinsic semiconductors;

9 describe an experiment which illustrates how the resistance of an *light dependent resistor* (LDR) varies with the intensity of light incident upon it;

10 describe an experiment which illustrates how the resistance of an *intrinsic semiconductor* varies with temperature;

11 explain why, in terms of band theory and the free-electron concentration in the conduction band, the conductivity of an intrinsic semiconductor increases with temperature;

12 show an appreciation of what is meant by a *superconducting* material;

13 recall that the electrical resistance of a superconducting material suddenly falls to zero at the *transition temperature* of that material;

14 outline the uses of superconducting materials, for example, in strong magnets;

15 describe an experiment which illustrates the *Hall effect*;

16 recall and use the equation $V_H = Bvd$ to calculate the *Hall voltage* V_H across a current-carrying conductor or semiconductor at right angles to a magnetic field;

17 describe how a calibrated *Hall probe* may be used to measure magnetic flux density.

Introduction

All materials have electrical properties but here we deal mainly with those materials which are useful in electrical or electronic engineering. Broadly speaking, electrical engineering is concerned with transferring and converting electrical energy while electronic engineering involves the systems which process, transmit and store information.

The electrical resistivity of a material is a characteristic property widely used in both branches of engineering. You were introduced to it in *Physics 1* and should recall that it has the symbol ρ and is defined by the equation

$$\rho = \frac{RA}{l}$$

R is the resistance of a sample of cross-sectional area A and length l. The units of resistivity are $\Omega\,\text{m}$.

Electrical conductivity

In *figure 2.1* the resistivities of solid materials are plotted on a logarithmic scale. You can see that the materials fall into three groups, with good insulators and good conductors at opposite ends of the scale and semiconductors in between. This chapter aims to explain the very large differences in resistivity along the scale in terms of electrons and their availability in solid materials. For this purpose it is helpful to use the property of conductivity rather than resistivity. The **conductivity** is simply the reciprocal of the resistivity. A conductivity scale is given in *figure 2.1* to make the relationship clear. The conductivity of a material is given the symbol σ (the Greek letter 'sigma').

$\sigma = 1/\rho$

σ is measured in $\Omega^{-1}\,\text{m}^{-1}$.

SAQ 2.1

The resistivity of silver is $1.60 \times 10^{-8}\,\Omega\text{m}$. What is its conductivity?

Drift velocity

Metals are good conductors because some of their electrons are free to flow through the metal under the influence of an electric field. *Figure 2.2* is a schematic representation of the structure of a metal. It shows a lattice of metal ions surrounded by a sea of free electrons. There are one, two or sometimes three free electrons for every metal ion.

Even when the metal is not carrying a current, the electrons are constantly in motion. They behave like the molecules in a gas, moving

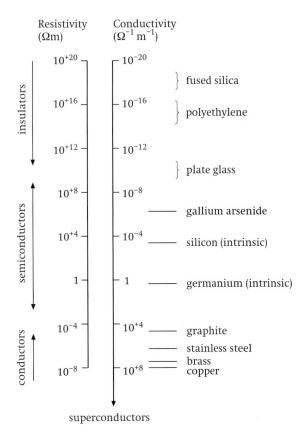

- **Figure 2.1** The range of resistivities and conductivities found in solid materials. The diagram shows how materials can be broadly classified as conductors, semiconductors or insulators.

- **Figure 2.2** A schematic illustration, in two dimensions, showing a lattice of metal ions (positive) in a 'sea' of electrons. Each metal ion vibrates about a fixed position. The free electrons do not have fixed positions; they are constantly in motion.

randomly in all directions. When they collide with the vibrating ions in the lattice they change speed and direction. If no current is flowing the average velocity of the electrons is zero. To describe the motion of the electrons we take their r.m.s. or **'root mean square'** speed. This is the square root of the average of the squares of the particle speeds. It is expressed mathematically as $\sqrt{<c^2>}$. The result has the dimensions of speed but is not equal to the average of the speeds themselves.

It is convenient to work with the r.m.s. value because it is closely related to the mean kinetic energy of the particles. For an individual molecule this is simply $\frac{1}{2}m<c^2>$. You will recall (*Physics 2* chapter 11) that the mean translational kinetic energy of a molecule of an ideal gas is proportional to the thermodynamic temperature. In *table 2.1* this relationship has been used to calculate values of the r.m.s. speed. The table shows the r.m.s. speed of an electron in an 'electron gas' along with typical values for other gases at a temperature of $0\,^{\circ}C$ ($T = 273\,K$). With an average speed of $10^5\,ms^{-1}$ the electrons are buzzing around very fast.

When a voltage is applied the force on the free electrons gives them an acceleration in the direction of the field. The motion they acquire is superimposed on their random movement with the result that, on average, they 'drift' in the direction of the field. *Figure 2.3* shows the path of an electron under the influence of an electric field. The electron is constantly changing velocity as it collides with the lattice but is being displaced at the same time. The average rate at which the electrons move in the direction of the field is the '**drift velocity**'. The net flow of electrons creates the current.

Gas	r.m.s. speed (ms^{-1}) at 0°C
Hydrogen (H_2)	1840
Helium (He)	1300
Oxygen (O_2)	650
Argon (Ar)	410
Electron gas	100 000

● **Table 2.1** Values for r.m.s speed at a temperature of $0\,^{\circ}C$ ($T = 273\,K$). The values are calculated for an ideal gas, using $\sqrt{<c^2>} = (3RT/M)^{\frac{1}{2}}$, where R is the universal gas constant, T is the thermodynamic temperature and M is the molar mass.

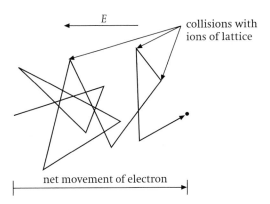

● **Figure 2.3** Schematic diagram showing the path of a free electron when a current, E, is flowing. It collides frequently with vibrating metal ions.

SAQ 2.2

a Explain why the net movement of the electron in *figure 2.3* is in a direction opposite to the direction of E, the applied electric field.

b Why do we talk about drift *velocity* rather than drift *speed*?

We will now see how the drift velocity is related to the current and estimate its value. You will see that it is very small compared with the r.m.s. speed.

Calculating the drift velocity

We start with a wire of cross-sectional area A carrying a current I (*figure 2.4*). The current is the rate at which charge flows through the wire. If a plane is drawn at right angles to the wire then the current is the amount of charge passing through this plane in one second. In a metal wire the moving charges are electrons travelling with a drift

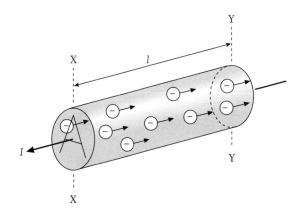

● **Figure 2.4** Electrons travelling through a metal wire.

velocity of v. We will need to know the number of free electrons in unit volume, this quantity is called the **number density** and is given the symbol n. e is the charge on an electron. The diagram shows a length l of wire. An electron in plane X will take time t to reach plane Y and, since v is the average velocity in this direction, we can write

$$v = \frac{l}{t}$$

In time t all the electrons between X and Y will also have passed through Y.

We can find how many by using n.

Number of electrons in section
XY = $n \times$ volume of section XY
= nlA

The amount of charge passing through Y will therefore be $nlAe$.

The current,

$$I = \frac{\text{amount of charge passing through Y}}{t}$$

$$= \frac{nlAe}{t}$$

As we already have $v = l/t$ this equation can be written as

$$I = nAve$$

Hint: You should be able to recall this equation. This is very easy if you remember it as the word spelt by the symbols.

Worked example

What is the drift velocity in copper when a current of 2.0 A is flowing through a wire of cross-sectional area $1.0 \times 10^{-6}\,\text{m}^2$? The number of free electrons in the copper is 8.5×10^{28} per cubic metre.

(The charge on an electron $e = -1.6 \times 10^{-19}$ C)

$I = nAve$

This equation can be rearranged to give

$$v = \frac{I}{nAe}$$

We have values for I, n, A and e so

$$v = \frac{2}{8.5 \times 10^{28} \times 1.0 \times 10^{-6} \times 1.6 \times 10^{-19}}$$

$$= 1.47 \times 10^{-4}\,\text{m}\,\text{s}^{-1}$$

Notice that, when we calculate a typical value it turns out to be very much smaller than the r.m.s. speed given in *table 2.1*.

SAQ 2.3
Use the result from the worked example above to estimate how long a single electron takes to travel along one metre of the same wire, carrying a 2 A current.

SAQ 2.4
Explain why, when you flick a light switch, the light goes on almost instantaneously even though the drift velocity of the electrons is approximately $1\,\text{mm}\,\text{s}^{-1}$.

The energy-band theory of solids

Our picture of the free electrons in a metal has allowed us to find a useful relationship. By using quantum mechanics, solid state physicists have gone beyond metals to model the properties of semiconductors and insulators. They have developed the **band theory** to describe the behaviour of electrons in most types of solid.

You have met line spectra (in *Physics 1*) and will know that the elements give sharp lines when they are in the form of a gas. This is because their atoms are far apart. Electrons in the isolated atom can only occupy certain levels of energy and, although they can be made to 'jump' from one energy level to another, they cannot sit at levels in between. One of the principles of quantum mechanics tells us that there can never be more than two electrons in one energy level. When the atoms are far apart each atom can have its electrons in identical energy levels. In a solid the distance between the atoms decreases and the outermost energy levels begin to overlap. Because the energy levels are the same for every atom the principle comes into action. To avoid violating it the levels split into very closely spaced energy levels. Their closeness means that they appear to merge into 'bands', which belong to the collection of atoms as a whole (*figure 2.5*).

The bands may overlap or there may be a gap between them where there are no energy levels at

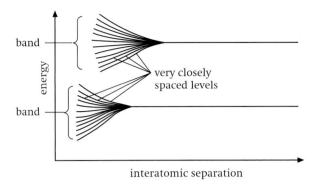

● **Figure 2.5** Energy levels and atomic separation: in a solid the levels split to form bands.

all. The actual distance between the atoms of a solid corresponds to their equilibrium separation, r_0. By taking the energy levels at this separation we can construct an energy level diagram to describe the band structure of the solid (*figure 2.6*).

SAQ 2.5

Figure 2.7 shows X-ray spectra emitted by solid aluminium and aluminium vapour when bombarded with electrons. The vapour spectrum shows sharp lines while the solid spectrum is continuous over a range of energy. Suggest a reason for the difference.

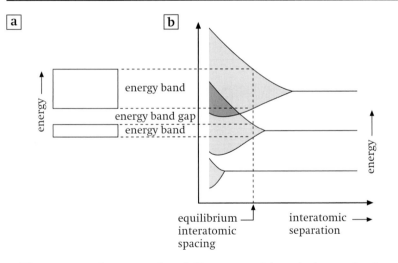

● **Figure 2.6 a** An energy band diagram and its relation to **b**, the curves showing energy levels against separation.

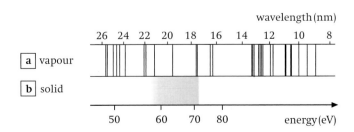

● **Figure 2.7** X-ray emission spectra for **a** aluminium vapour and **b** solid aluminium.

Conduction in metals

We already think of a metal as a lattice of positive ions surrounded by a sea of free electrons. *Figure 2.8* shows how the orbitals of outermost electrons overlap, becoming fuzzy as they split into a band of very closely spaced energy levels. The electrons in the overlapping orbitals are said to be 'delocalised' because they can move from one orbit to the next. This happens when a current flows.

Figure 2.9 overleaf shows the band structure in a metal. It has one, partially filled band which contains the free electrons responsible for electrical conductivity. For this reason it is known as the **conduction band**. You may find it called the 'conductance - valence band' in other books. This is because the electrons in this band also bind the lattice together in the metallic bond.

When a potential difference is applied across the metal a current starts to flow and the conduction electrons are given a small amount of energy. At first sight our 'drift velocity' model of conductivity might appear to break the rules of quantum theory as it allows the moving electrons to gain and lose energy in a continuous fashion.

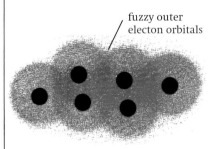

● **Figure 2.8** Overlapping of outer electron orbitals.

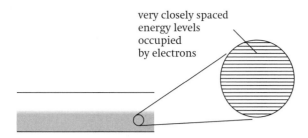

● **Figure 2.9** The conduction band in a metal. The shading indicates that the levels are very close together and that the band is only partially filled.

Quantum theory tells us that their energy can only change in 'jumps' between certain levels. In fact there is no conflict if you remember that the band is actually made up of very finely spaced energy levels. The electrons hop from one level to another as their energies change.

It is important to appreciate that the energy band is only partially full as this means that there are plenty of empty levels. When the conduction electrons acquire energy they move up to occupy levels in the previously empty part of the conduction band.

In semiconductors and insulators there is an **energy gap** between the valence band and the conduction band. It is very significant in explaining their conductivity. But we must first look at the charge carriers in these materials.

The charge carriers in semiconductors

Silicon, germanium and gallium arsenide are typical semiconductors. They have the same crystal structure as diamond (*figure 2.10*). *Figure 2.11a* is a two-dimensional representation of the silicon

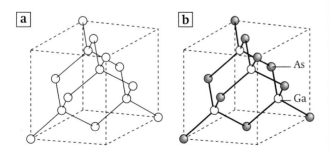

● **Figure 2.10 a** The crystal structure of diamond, silicon and germanium; **b** the crystal structure of gallium arsenide.

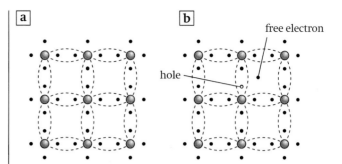

● **Figure 2.11 a** The crystal structure of silicon. The bonds are shown in two-dimensions. **b** A valence electron escapes from a bond leaving a 'positive hole'.

structure. Each atom has four electrons (shown as dots) in its outer shell. Neighbouring atoms share these electrons (sometimes called the valence electrons) to form covalent bonds.

Figure 2.11b shows how the material conducts. A few electrons have enough energy to free themselves from the bonds. The number escaping is very small, in pure silicon at room temperature it is less than one in a billion. The escaped electrons then behave like the conduction electrons in a metal. Because the number of free electrons is very small compared with the number in a metal the conductivity is very much lower.

The escaping electron leaves a vacant site in the structure (*figure 2.11b*) and, because the electron takes negative charge with it, the site it leaves behind has a positive charge. It is therefore known as a 'positive hole' and can act like a charge +*e*.

An electron from a neighbouring bond can move into the empty site, creating a positive hole at another site in the lattice. In effect the holes can move through the lattice carrying positive charge with them. In the absence of an electric field free electrons and positive holes move at random through the crystal. When a potential difference is applied across the crystal the negative electrons and the positive holes 'drift' independently and in opposite directions through the material.

SAQ 2.6

In pure silicon the free electrons carry about 75% of the current. Explain how this can happen, given that there are equal numbers of free electrons and positive holes.

In a pure semiconductor all the charge carriers originate from the material itself. It is said to be an **intrinsic semiconductor**.

Band structure of intrinsic semiconductors

The band structure of a typical intrinsic semiconductor is shown in *figure 2.12*. The shared electrons occupy the **valence band** while above this lies the conduction band. Between the bands there is a gap, sometimes called the 'forbidden' gap because electrons can never have energies within it. When a valence electron acquires an energy greater than the gap energy it can escape from its bond and jump into the conduction band. The conduction band is almost empty so that, when an electric field is applied, the electron can gain a little more energy and move through the crystal. At room temperature just a few electrons have enough energy to escape into the conduction band.

An intrinsic semiconductor has one hole in the valence band for each electron in the conduction band. Occasionally a conduction electron falls into a positive hole, in a process known as recombination. At a given temperature the rate at which electrons escape is equal to the rate at which they recombine so that the number of electrons in the conduction band stays constant. *Table 2.2* gives values for the number densities of free electrons and positive holes in pure silicon, germanium and gallium arsenide at 300 K. Notice that the number density of free electrons equals the number density of positive holes.

Intrinsic semiconductor	number of charge carriers per m^3	
	Electrons	**Positive holes**
Silicon	1.4×10^{16}	1.4×10^{16}
Germanium	2.4×10^{19}	2.4×10^{19}
Gallium arsenide	1.7×10^{12}	1.7×10^{12}

● **Table 2.2** Number densities of free electrons and positive holes in intrinsic semiconductors at 300 K.

Contrast these numbers with the value for a good conductor, where a typical value of the number density would be 10^{28} free electrons per m^3. The difference explains why the conductivity of a semiconductor is many powers of 10 less than that of a metal.

SAQ 2.7

Explain why, in *table 2.2*, the number density of electrons is equal to the number density of positive holes.

Band structure of insulators

The band structure of an insulator is similar to that of an intrinsic semi-conductor except in the size of the gap between the valence and conduction band (*figure 2.13*).

In a semiconductor the gap is relatively small (<2 eV) while in an insulator it is larger (>2 eV). The valence band in an insulator is full and the electrons do not, at normal temperatures, have enough energy to jump into the conduction band. Because it has no charge carriers the material cannot conduct.

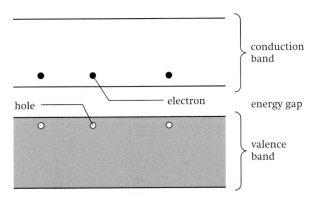

● **Figure 2.12** The valence and conduction bands in an intrinsic semiconductor. At room temperature a few electrons have escaped into the conduction band. They leave 'positive holes' in the valence band, which is otherwise full of electrons.

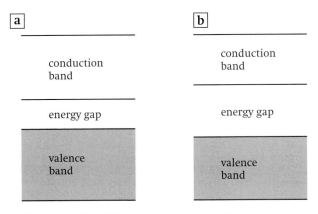

● **Figure 2.13 a** The band structure of a semiconductor compared with **b** that of an insulator.

The effect of light and heat on semiconductors

You will remember from *Physics 1* that the resistivity of a metal increases with temperature. This happens because the increasing vibrations of the metal ions makes it less easy for the electrons to move through the lattice. Semiconductors respond to an increase in temperature in the opposite way. We now explore the effect of both light and heat in two experiments.

Investigating the effect of light on a light dependent resistor (LDR)

Figure 2.14b shows the circuit you need to set up. A typical LDR (light dependent resistor) is shown in the inset. The window through which light reaches the resistor also allows you to see its structure. The semiconducting material lies between two sets of interleaved 'fingers' of gold which connect it to the external circuit.

The multimeter is switched to its 'ohms × 1 k' range. Vary the amount of light falling on the LDR (you can simply cover and uncover it) and note how its resistance changes. You will see that the resistance falls as the illumination increases. You can calibrate the LDR in units of lux by comparing the readings with those of a commercial light meter. The curve will not be linear (*figure 2.14c*).

Remember that, in this mode, the multimeter is using its internal battery. Do not leave it on unnecessarily! You may prefer to use a potential divider circuit to measure resistances (see *Physics 1* pages 109–11).

You may also try investigating the response of the photocell to light of different wavelengths. This can be done using filters or by forming a spectrum from white light and moving the LDR through it. There should be a response across the visible spectrum (*figure 2.14d*).

Guide to source illuminations

Light sources	Illumination (Lux)
Moonlight	0.1
60 W bulb at 1 m	50
1 W MES bulb at 0.1 m	100
Fluorescent lighting	500
Bright sunlight	30 000

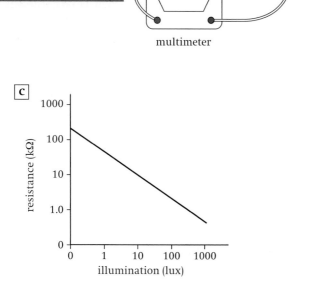

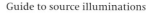

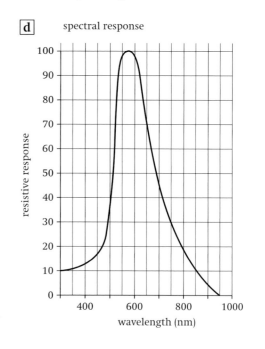

● **Figure 2.14**
a A light dependent resistor (NORP 12).
b Measuring the resistance of the LDR using a multimeter.
c Graph showing typical values of resistance against illumination.
d The spectral response of the LDR. This is similar to that of the human eye.

Investigating the effect of heat on an NTC thermistor

Thermistors of this type are made from semiconducting metal oxides. Their resistance decreases with temperature. They are called NTC (negative temperature coefficient) to distinguish them from a less common type, PTC (positive temperature coefficient) where the resistance of the thermistor increases with temperature.

The most direct way to investigate the effect uses a multimeter, switched to its resistance range. The set up is shown in *figure 2.15a*. Again, a potential divider circuit may be used instead. The diagram shows how to measure the resistance whilst temperature varies. Provided the water is distilled or deionised the conductivity of the water will not affect the measurements. Typical results for a readily available, inexpensive type of NTC thermistor are shown in *figure 2.15b*.

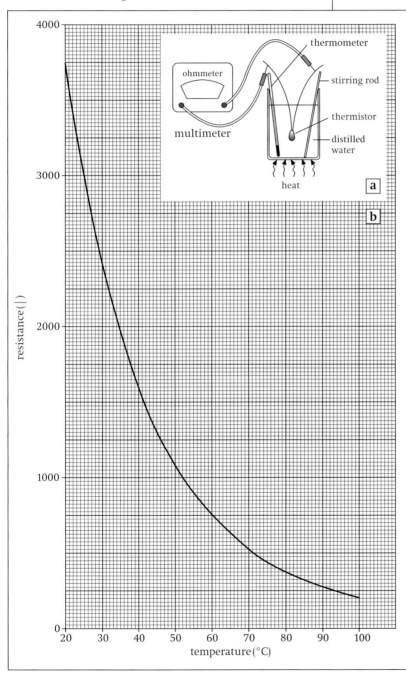

SAQ 2.8
Look at the graph in *figure 2.15b*. Over what range of temperature is R varying rapidly? Why would this make the thermistor especially useful as a temperature probe over this range?

Using band theory to explain the results

The effect of light
When the semiconductor material of the LDR is illuminated it is able to take in energy. The light supplies some of the electrons in the valence band with enough energy to jump the forbidden gap and enter the conduction band. Once there they are free to carry charge. As they leave the valence band they create positive holes which also act as charge carriers. Because more charge carriers are now available the conductivity of the material goes up.

To be useful as a light sensor an LDR should respond to wavelengths across the visible spectrum. The semiconductor commonly used in LDRs is cadmium sulphide but the material is not in its pure or intrinsic form. Instead, it is extrinsic which means that it contains very small quantities of other atoms, added by a process called **doping**. Extrinsic semiconductors are outside the scope of the present book but are briefly

● **Figure 2.15**
a A set-up for investigating the effect of temperature on the resistance, R, of an NTC thermistor.
b Results obtained for RS thermistor 151–215.

introduced in *box 2.2*. Photons in the visible spectrum have energies between about 1.8 eV and 3.1 eV. Intrinsic cadmium sulphide has a band gap of 2.4 eV so that a sensor made of this material could not absorb photons of energy lower than 2.4 eV (wavelengths longer than 0.52 μm). The effect of the impurity atoms is to reduce the band gap to about 1.7 eV with the result that the extrinsic cadmium sulphide can absorb photons with energies at the lower limit of the visible range. The connection between band gap, the absorption of photons and wavelength will be discussed in more detail in chapter 4.

The effect of heat

As the NTC thermistor is heated its internal energy increases. With an increase in temperature, more valence electrons have sufficient energy to escape into the conduction band. As a result the number of free electrons and the number of positive holes increases. Although the increase in temperature slightly reduces the rate at which charge carriers travel through the lattice, the increase in their number has an overwhelming effect and the conductivity goes up.

If the size of the energy gap is known it is possible to predict how the population of the conduction band will increase with temperature.

When a graph obtained with intrinsic silicon (*figure 2.16a*) is analysed it shows that the increase in the occupancy of the conduction band largely accounts for the results.

SAQ 2.9

Explain the following facts:

a Diamond has an energy band gap of about 5 eV. At very high temperatures it becomes an electrical conductor.

b Intrinsic silicon is an insulator at very low temperatures.

Superconductivity

A superconductor is a material which, below a certain **transition temperature**, conducts with no resistance at all. Zero resistance is a most useful property since no energy is lost when a current flows. The temperature below which a material exhibits superconductivity is sometimes referred to as the critical temperature. The fall in resistance at this temperature is very sharp. The phenomenon of superconductivity was discovered in the first decade of the twentieth century but leapt to prominence in 1986. The transition temperatures for the superconductors discovered before then could only be

a

[Graph: conductivity ($\Omega^{-1}m^{-1}$) on the y-axis ranging from 0 to 1200, versus temperature (°C) on the x-axis ranging from 300 to 700. The curve rises exponentially from near zero at 300 °C to about 1200 at 700 °C.]

● **Figure 2.16**

a The temperature dependence of the conductivity of intrinsic silicon. (Adapted from the results of G. L. Pearson and J. Bardeen.)

b The transistor was invented in 1947 by Bardeen, Brattain and Shockley (left to right). They are shown here at a banquet held in their honour in 1977.

Box 2.2 Extrinsic semiconductors

The electronics industry uses semiconductor materials to fabricate integrated circuits. The semiconductors in these devices are extrinsic semiconductors, so-called because their conductivity is due mainly to the presence of extra charge carriers derived from minute concentrations of impurities. In *n*-type semiconductors the extra charge carriers are electrons (negative) while in *p*-type semiconductors the extra charge carriers are positive holes. In both cases the conductivity is very much higher than that of the pure material because there are many more free charge carriers.

In a crystal of silicon or germanium each atom shares four electrons with neighbouring atoms to form four covalent bonds (*Figure 2.11a*). Extra free electrons (or holes) are introduced into an extrinsic semiconductor by replacing a very small number of atoms in the lattice with atoms which have either five or three valence electrons. This process is known as doping.

Figure 2.17 shows how this works for an *n*-type semiconductor. A phosphorus atom, for example, with one extra valence electron, replaces a silicon atom in the lattice. The extra electron is not part of the bonds that hold the lattice together. It does not take much energy to free it from the phosphorus atom. Once free it can move through the crystal leaving behind a positively charged phosphorus ion. In energy level terms, the extra free electrons introduce energy levels within the band gap. It therefore takes less energy to kick the electrons up into the conduction band. As a result the doped crystal has a much higher conductivity at room temperature than pure silicon.

Figure 2.18 shows the corresponding picture for a *p*-type semiconductor. Trivalent atoms (e.g. indium) introduce extra positive holes. New energy levels appear in the band gap and have the effect of making more positive holes available to carry charge at room temperature.

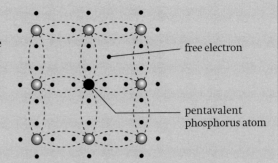

● **Figure 2.17** An *n*-type semiconductor. The 'dopant' has five valence electrons. One of these electrons becomes a free electron.

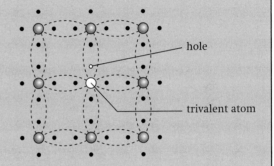

● **Figure 2.18** A *p*-type semiconductor. The dopant has only three valence electrons. This creates an extra positive hole.

reached using liquid helium. In 1986, materials with transition temperatures above the boiling point of liquid nitrogen were discovered. Liquid nitrogen is much cheaper to use than liquid helium so these **high-temperature superconductors** were seen to have great technological potential. The evolution of superconductors is shown in *figure 2.19*. The new high-temperature superconductors are ceramics. Bednorz and Muller were awarded the Nobel prize for their work on these materials.

The first Nobel prize in the field of superconductivity was won by the Dutch physicist Kammerlingh Onnes. In 1911 he measured the resistance of a fine thread of very pure mercury and found that it dropped to zero at 4.15 K. The fall in resistance happens abruptly, as you can see from the curve (*figure 2.20*).

A theory developed by Bardeen, Cooper and Schrieffer, known from their initials as the BCS theory, explains very-low-temperature conductivity. You have seen that the conductivity of metals and

alloys falls with increasing temperature because the lattice vibrations increase and hinder the flow of charge. In the superconducting state the charge

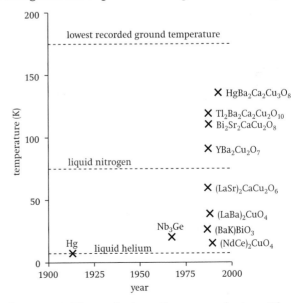

● **Figure 2.19** The evolution of superconductors. The transition temperature of the superconductor is plotted against the year of its discovery.

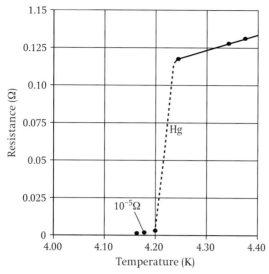

● **Figure 2.20** Graph of the resistance of mercury as it cools, from Kammerlingh Onnes' notebook.

carriers are thought to move with the lattice vibrations in a concerted process, so that there is no resistance. Above the transition temperature the lattice vibrations become too strong and disrupt the delicate interactions involved.

The mechanism of superconductivity in high-temperature superconductors is still being researched. An example of one of these compounds is shown in *figure 2.21*. It is thought that the crystalline structure allows charge to travel easily along certain planes.

Applications of superconductivity

When a superconductor is placed in a magnetic field the result can be very striking. In *figure 2.22* a block of yttrium barium copper oxide which has been cooled by liquid nitrogen is floating above a

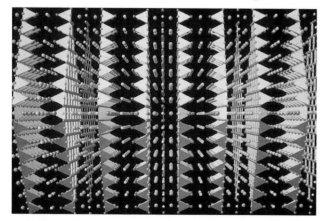

● **Figure 2.21** At 135 K this superconductor has the highest transition temperature yet known. It contains layers of mercury, barium, calcium, copper and oxide ions stacked in a regular sequence.

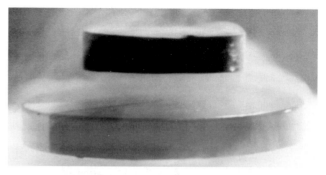

● **Figure 2.22** After cooling in liquid nitrogen a block of yttrium barium copper oxide levitates above a magnet.

magnet. This happens because the magnetic field causes currents to flow in the superconductor. There is no resistance, so the charges are in 'perpetual motion'. These currents in the super-conductor set up a magnetic field which exactly opposes the applied field. The result is a strong repulsive force powerful enough to levitate the magnet.

The effect has been used for the transport of people. The Japanese have developed a train that floats on strong superconducting magnets, eliminating friction between the train and its tracks. Without friction the train can reach extremely high speeds. In 1999 a train on the Yamanashi test line (*figure 2.23*) achieved a speed of 552 km per hour.

On a smaller scale superconductors are used in electronic devices. One of the best known applications is called a SQUID (*figure 2.24*). The letters stand for 'superconducting quantum interference device'. A squid can be used as an extremely sensitive device for measuring magnetic fields. It can detect the minute magnetic fields from electrical impulses in living organisms. In

● **Figure 2.23** The Yamanashi test line.

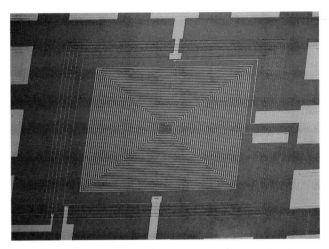

● **Figure 2.24** A scanning electron micrograph of a SQUID, the most sensitive magnetic detector known.

medicine squids can measure foetal heartbeats and detect electrical activity in the brain.

Superconductors are beginning to be used in cellular telephone systems as filters. An ideal filter selects a single frequency, but in practice resistance causes a filter to tune to a range of frequencies. A superconducting filter, with zero resistance, is closer to the ideal and should, therefore, be able to pick up a signal in a very crowded spectrum. It also has the advantage of consuming less power so that it does not diminish the signal and, as a result, weaker signals can be sent from the aerial to the receiver.

The Hall effect

A current flowing in a conductor or semiconductor can be deflected by a magnetic field in just the same way as a beam of electrons in a fine-beam tube (*Physics 2*). E. H. Hall discovered the effect in 1879 and it is named after him.

In *figure 2.25a* a current passes along the length of a rectangular slice of material. The width of the slice is *d*. Here the charge carriers are pictured as electrons with a drift velocity *v* which carries them in the opposite direction to the current. A magnetic field with flux density *B* acts in a direction at right angles to the plane of the slice. This field exerts a force on the

moving charges. If you apply Fleming's left-hand rule you will be able to predict that they are deflected in the direction shown. They crowd towards one edge of the plate leaving the other edge depleted. The result is that one edge becomes negatively charged and the other positive. A voltmeter connected across the edges detects a potential difference. This is the **Hall voltage** V_H. It depends on the magnitudes of B, v and d and is given by the equation

$$V_H = Bvd$$

The corresponding picture for positive charge is shown in *figure 2.25b*. Here the drift velocity is in the opposite direction. You can again use Fleming's left hand rule to predict the deflection. It will be in the *same* direction as for the negative charge carriers but the build up of charge will lead to a Hall voltage of the opposite sign.

In an intrinsic semiconductor, where the number of free electrons equals the number of positive holes, the Hall voltage due to the negative and positive charges will more or less cancel out. It can be readily detected, however, in *n*- and *p*-type extrinsic semiconductors, because they contain large excesses of either negative or positive charge carriers. The sign of the Hall voltage indicates whether the semiconductor is *n*-type or *p*-type. The magnitude of the voltage can be used to calculate the concentration of the charge carriers.

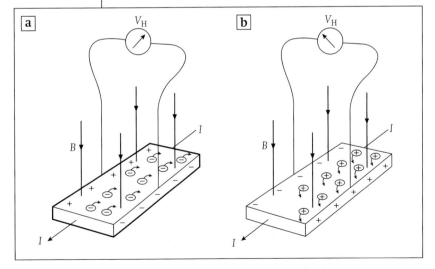

● **Figure 2.25** The Hall effect. A magnetic field deflects moving charges in a slice of solid material; this effect produces a voltage at right angles to the field and the current. In **a** the charge carriers are electrons and in **b** they are positive holes. The potential difference measured in **a** is of the opposite sign to that measured in **b**.

SAQ 2.10

Explain why V_H tends to be much bigger in semiconductors than in metals. (*Hint*: think about drift velocities.)

Demonstrating the Hall effect

Figure 2.26 shows a circuit board designed to demonstrate the **Hall effect**. Look for the rectangular slice of germanium and identify the terminals through which the current enters and leaves the slice, and those for connecting a voltmeter to measure the Hall voltage. This board is one of a set of two. A slice of *n*-type germanium, doped so that it contains an excess of negative charge carriers, is mounted on one. The slice on the other board is *p*-type germanium, with an excess of positive holes.

A bar magnet, brought near the surface of one of the wafers, will produce a Hall voltage which can be measured using a millivoltmeter. (Be careful not to let the magnet touch the wafer as this would damage the semiconductor.) The sign of the Hall voltage will be reversed if you repeat the measurement with the other type of extrinsic semiconductor.

To test the relationship between B and V_H the slice can be mounted between a pair of Helmholtz coils. The magnetic field in the space between the coils is very uniform and it is possible to calculate the flux density (see *Physics 2*, chapter 9).

Calculating the Hall voltage

We can use the equation $V_H = Bvd$ to predict the size of the Hall voltage in the demonstration. First

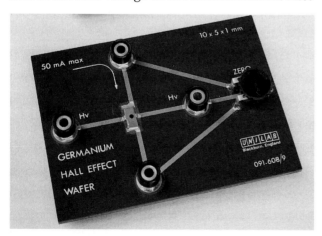

● **Figure 2.26** Circuit board designed to demonstrate the Hall effect.

we need to estimate the drift velocity, v.

In the circuit board shown in *figure 2.26* the current flows through a slice of semiconductor 5 mm wide and 1 mm thick. Suppose that the slice is made from an *n*-type semiconductor doped to contain 8.0×10^{20} negative charge charges per cubic metre. If we set the current at 20 mA we can calculate the drift velocity v using the formula on page 30:

$$I = nAve$$

We can rearrange this as

$$v = \frac{I}{nAe}$$

A is $5.0\,\text{mm}^2$ and we have values for I and n. The magnitude of the charge on an electron, e, is $1.6 \times 10^{-19}\text{C}$. Substituting gives

$$v = \frac{20 \times 10^{-3}}{8.0 \times 10^{20} \times 5.0 \times 10^{-6} \times 1.6 \times 10^{-19}}$$

$$= 31.0\,\text{m s}^{-1}$$

Now that we have a value for v we can use the equation $V_H = Bvd$ to calculate the Hall voltage. If B is 0.2 T then

$$V_H = 0.2 \times 31.0 \times 5.0 \times 10^{-3}$$

$$= 0.031\,\text{V}$$

$$= 31\,\text{mV}$$

In metals the Hall effect is very much smaller. This is because the concentration of free electrons in a metal is, at about $10^{28}\,\text{m}^{-3}$, much higher than in a semiconductor. If the calculation is repeated for a slice of metal with the same dimensions then, even for a current of 3 A, the drift velocity is only $3.8 \times 10^{-4}\,\text{m s}^{-1}$. In a large magnetic field the Hall voltage will be measured in microvolts.

SAQ 2.11

a Use the above value of $3.8 \times 10^{-4}\,\text{m s}^{-1}$ for the drift velocity in a slice of metal, width 5.0 mm, to estimate the Hall voltage in a strong magnetic field of 2.2 Teslas.

b Hall discovered the effect named after him in 1879 but it only found application a century later. Why was this?

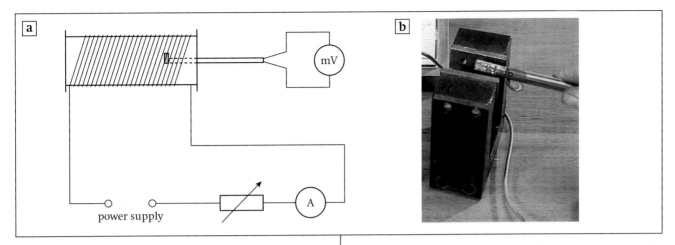

● **Figure 2.27**
a Investigation of B inside a solenoid using a Hall probe.
b The Hall probe is mounted on a ball and socket joint.

Using a Hall probe

Wafers of semiconductor are used to make **Hall probes** to sense and track magnetic fields. In the probe in the photograph (*figure 2.27b*) the wafer is mounted on a ball and socket joint attached to a handle. The probe is calibrated at the factory so that the meter measures the magnetic flux density in tesla. Such probes are sensitive enough to measure the Earth's magnetic flux density . In the British Isles this is about 4×10^{-5} T. They can also be used to measure the tilt of the Earth's magnetic field (the angle of dip).

Figure 2.27a shows the Hall probe set up to measure the *B*-field inside a solenoid. Notice that the wafer is positioned so that it is in a plane perpendicular to the field.

SUMMARY

◆ Electrical conductivity is defined as the reciprocal of electrical resistivity: $\sigma = 1/\rho$. The units are $\Omega^{-1}\,m^{-1}$.

◆ When a single charge carrier gives rise to a current, it has a drift velocity, *v*, which is related to the current by the equation $I = nAve$.

◆ The drift velocity of an electron in a metal is very small compared with the r.m.s. speed of its random motion in an electron gas.

◆ In a solid material the outermost energy levels of neighbouring atoms merge to form bands.

◆ In a metal the free electrons occupy the conduction band. Because the band is only partially full the electrons are able to move between energy levels within the band and so form an electric current.

◆ In semiconductors and insulators there is an energy gap between the conduction band and the valence band. Electrons cannot have energies within this band gap.

◆ At normal temperatures a few electrons in the valence band of an intrinsic semiconductor have enough energy to cross the band gap and occupy the conduction band.

◆ Insulators have a larger band gap than semiconductors. Under normal conditions electrons are unable to escape into the conduction band and so it is empty.

◆ The occupancy or otherwise of the conduction band explains the huge differences in conductivity between metals, semiconductors and insulators.

- When the temperature of an intrinsic semiconductor rises, more electrons acquire sufficient energy to enter the conduction band. This causes an increase in conductivity.

- At low temperatures some materials become superconductors. At the transition temperature their resistance falls suddenly to zero.

- The charges carrying a current in a solid material are deflected by a magnetic field. This is the Hall effect.

- The Hall voltage V_H is related to the drift velocity v of the charge carriers by the equation $V_H = Bvd$

Questions

1 a Define electrical conductivity.

b The electrical conductivity of platinum is $1.02 \times 10^{-8}\ \Omega^{-1}\,m^{-1}$. What length of wire diameter 0.076 mm is required to give a resistance of 25 Ω?

2 The current I flowing through a wire is related to the drift velocity v of the free electrons in the wire by:

$I = nAve$

where A is the cross-sectional area of the wire and e is the electronic charge.

a By considering a section of wire of length v metres (or otherwise), derive this relationship.

b By referring to the relationship above, explain why electron drift velocities in semiconductors are typically much higher than those of free electrons in metals.

3 A current of 1.0 A passes through a copper wire of diameter 0.457 mm. Calculate the magnitude of the drift velocity of the free electrons in the wire, given that their concentration is $8.7 \times 10^{28}\,m^{-3}$. The charge on a free electron is -1.60×10^{-19} C.

4 When light falls on a light dependent resistor (LDR), its conductivity increases.

a Describe an experiment to demonstrate this. Include a circuit diagram in your answer.

b An LDR is made from a semiconducting material. When a photon of light strikes the semiconductor, an electron may move from the valence band to the conduction band. Draw a diagram of the energy bands of a semiconductor to illustrate this process. Explain why this increases the conductivity of the semiconductor.

5 A strong magnet may be made by winding a coil (or solenoid) of superconducting wire.

a Why must the coil be cooled for use as a magnet?

b What advantages does such a magnet have over other strong electromagnets?

c Suggest two different uses for such a superconducting magnet.

6 The Hall voltage V_H across a conductor or semiconductor in a magnetic field of flux density B is given by:

$V_H = Bvd$

a State the meanings of the terms v and d in this relationship.

b Describe how the Hall effect may be used to measure magnetic flux density.

c Referring to the equation above, explain why a Hall probe is made using a slice of a semiconducting material, rather than a metal.

CHAPTER 3

Magnetic properties of materials

By the end of this chapter you should be able to:

1 use the *domain theory* of magnetism to describe the macroscopic magnetic properties of *ferromagnetic* materials;

2 use the domain theory to distinguish between hard and soft ferromagnetic materials;

3 recall that a material which is fully magnetised has reached saturation;

4 sketch and interpret graphical representations of the variation of the magnetic flux density within a material with the flux density causing *magnetisation* in an initially unmagnetised material;

5 explain what is meant by *magnetic hysteresis*;

6 sketch and interpret graphical representations of *magnetic hysteresis loops* for both soft and hard ferromagnetic materials;

7 recall that the magnetic alignment of dipoles is completely disrupted at the *Curie temperature* of a given material;

8 use the ideas of hysteresis loops, *saturation flux densities*, the movement of *domain walls* and the presence of *eddy currents*, to explain how energy losses from the core of a transformer affect the efficiency of the transformer;

9 appreciate that new materials with energy-efficient *microstructures* have been developed for the cores of some transformers, for example metallic glass which is easy to magnetise in all directions;

10 describe an experiment which illustrates how the efficiency of a transformer varies with the frequency of the supply;

11 explain, with reference to *Faraday's law* of electromagnetic induction, why energy losses caused by eddy currents in the core of a transformer depend upon the frequency of the supply.

Introduction

The magnetic compass was discovered in China. A book from 1044 AD gives the first description of a practical navigation instrument, in the form of a cup-shaped iron fish floating on water (*figure 3.1*). The compass-fish was magnetised by being heated to red heat and then cooled while held in a North-South position in the Earth's magnetic field. The Chinese had known about magnetic polarity, the property on which compasses depend, a thousand years earlier than this. They had made magnetic pointers from magnetite, a magnetic iron ore.

● **Figure 3.1**
Floating iron compass-fish. The diagram is a reconstruction based on a book of military techniques written in 1044 AD.

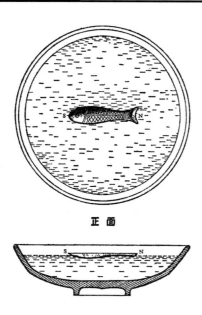

正 面

● **Figure 3.2** A scanning electron micrograph showing the microstructure of a floppy disc. Tiny needle-shaped permanent magnets are embedded in a resin. × 11 500

Believing magnetism to be a supernatural power they had used these devices not for navigation but for divination and magic.

To this day we find magnets fascinating, but now we have theories to explain magnetism in terms of electrons and atoms. In this chapter you use ideas from these theories to explore the connections between magnetic properties and the microstructures of magnetic materials.

Modern technology has found many applications for magnetic materials. In electrical engineering they are used in electric motors, generators and transformers. In this chapter we will be focussing on their use in transformer cores. Other types of magnetic material are of great importance in storing information. *Figure 3.2* shows the tiny needle-shaped permanent magnets that record data on a floppy disc. The needles can only be magnetised along their length, in one direction or the opposite. This makes it possible to record information in digital form, as ones and noughts. Each needle stays magnetised after the recording field has gone, allowing the disc to 'remember' information.

Ferromagnetic materials

Ferromagnetic materials include iron, cobalt, nickel and the rare-earth element gadolinium. They can be strongly magnetised and the magnetism may remain even after the magnetising field

is removed; many permanent magnets are made from these materials. We begin with a close look at the origin of magnetic properties at the level of atomic structure. We will deal with the question of just how the properties are described and measured later in this chapter. There is a good reason for seeking to understand the underlying mechanisms: it enables us to predict how changes in structure will affect magnetic behaviour. This makes it possible to alter the properties and, in some cases, make magnetic materials with properties to order.

The origin of magnetic force

There is no fundamental difference between the ways in which a permanent magnet and a current-carrying coil create a magnetic field. You met this idea in *Physics 1* and will be able to sketch the fields. In *figure 3.3* the magnetic field around a current loop is shown, together with that of a bar magnet. The poles of the bar magnet are labelled North and South while an arrow on the loop indicates the direction of the current. You can see that the fields are very similar. Both can be described by the term 'magnetic dipole'. It is convenient to simplify such diagrams by representing a dipole as an arrow. The arrow points in the direction of the field. Both fields have the same origin. They arise because charges are moving. In *box 3.1* you can read more about the origin of magnetic fields.

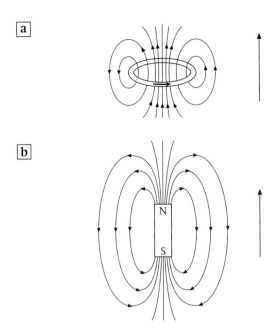

● **Figure 3.3** The magnetic fields around **a** a loop carrying a current and **b** a bar magnet. The arrow on the loop represents the direction of the conventional current. Both are magnetic dipoles and can be represented by an arrow drawn in the direction of the field lines along the axes.

SAQ 3.1

Draw a current loop with the current circulating in the opposite direction to that in *figure 3.3*. Draw an arrow to represent the dipole associated with it.

Atomic dipoles

In a magnetic material the moving charges are electrons. *Figure 3.4a* shows a single electron in orbit in the space surrounding the nucleus. Although the motion produces a magnetic dipole this contributes very little to the overall magnetic field in a solid. This is because orbital-motion effects due to the different electrons in an atom tend to cancel each other out. The source of the strong magnetism in ferromagnetic materials is electron spin.

In *figure 3.4b* the electron is shown as a spinning sphere. It acts like a minute current which circulates in a loop and produces a magnetic dipole. The sphere has an axis and can spin in a clockwise or anticlockwise direction. An arrow is used to represent the two spin directions. When two electrons with opposite spins are paired their magnetism exactly cancels out. In most elements

Box 3.1 Relativity and electricity

Magnetic fields were once thought to be quite distinct from electrostatic fields. Einstein was convinced that this was not so. In a letter, written in 1952, he said

'What led me more or less directly to the special theory of relativity was the conviction that the electromotive force acting on a body in motion in a magnetic field was nothing else but an electric field.'
(Letter to the Michelson Commemorative Meeting of the Cleveland Physics Society as quoted by R.S.Shankland, Am. J. Phys., **32**, 16 (1964), p.35.)

Einstein investigated the effect of a uniformly moving source charge upon a moving test charge. He showed that relativity predicts an extra force between them on top of that due to electrostatic attraction. This is the magnetic force. In the last chapter we saw that the current in a wire is carried by electrons moving with a drift velocity of less than one millimetre per second. This motion is enough to create the magnetic field around a wire. Many people suppose that velocities have to be close to the speed of light for relativity to be important, but this is not the case. We will not take relativistic ideas further here, although more can be learned about them in another book in this series (*Cosmology*, Chapter 6).

the inner energy levels of the atoms are completely full. Each contains equal numbers of electrons with opposite spins so that none remain unpaired. We have seen (chapter 2) that the conduction band in a metal contains single electrons. But the spin dipole of one electron is very small and, since they are 'free' and therefore unaligned, these electrons do not contribute to the

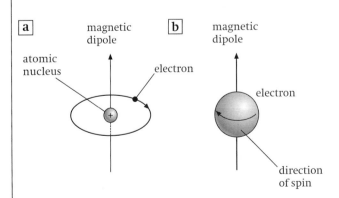

● **Figure 3.4**
a The magnetic dipole due to an electron moving in an orbit.
b A spinning electron produces a dipole.

magnetism of the solid. In iron, nickel and cobalt, which are ferromagnetic, each atom retains some unpaired electrons; iron atoms, for instance, have an average of about two. Their effects combine to give the atom an 'atomic dipole moment'. These unpaired electrons sit in a partly filled outer energy level of the atom, leaving others to escape into the conduction band.

Why, then, are so few metals ferromagnetic? Other metals have unpaired outer electrons in their energy levels. You will know that manganese and chromium are not ferromagnetic and yet they have similar electron structures to iron. To produce strong magnetism there has to be a coupling interaction between the magnetic dipoles of neighbouring atoms. This causes the dipoles to align with one another. They then act in unison to produce a magnetic field. The coupling force arises because the unpaired electrons in fact 'time-share' between the atomic orbitals and the conductance band. *Figure 3.5* shows the alignment of the atomic dipoles in a ferromagnetic material. There is no external magnetic field to bring about the alignment. It happens spontaneously and extends through relatively large regions of the crystal called **domains**. A single domain contains billions of atoms.

Domains

Weiss put forward the domain theory in 1907, two decades before there was an explanation for atomic magnets. He was answering the question 'How can a single magnetic material gain or lose magnetism?' He proposed that a ferromagnetic material is divided into small regions, each of which is completely magnetised. These regions are the **domains**. The diagram in *figure 3.6* is a

● **Figure 3.6** Two-dimensional representation of the domains in a ferromagnetic material. In each domain all the atomic dipoles are aligned but the material as a whole has no magnetism.

two-dimensional representation of his idea. The arrows represent atomic magnets. Although at that time he could have had no notion of electron spin, Weiss was using the concept of an atomic dipole. The sample in the diagram is not magnetised. Each domain has magnetisation but the size of the domains and the different directions of the atomic magnets combine to produce zero net magnetisation of the sample.

The boundaries between the domains are known as **domain walls**. A wall is made up of several layers of atoms through which the atomic dipoles change direction (*figure 3.7*). Domains were

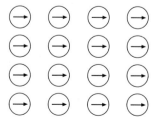

● **Figure 3.5** Schematic diagram showing the alignment of atomic magnets in a single domain in a ferromagnetic material. There may or may not be an external field.

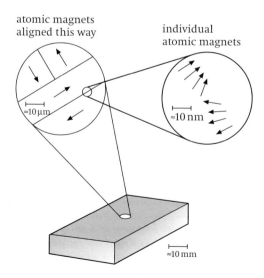

● **Figure 3.7** A domain wall in a sample of unmagnetised iron.

eventually made visible (*figure 3.8a* and *b*). The scale on the images shows that they are relatively large. The images were obtained using the two different techniques described in *box 3.2*.

Although very small particles can exist as single domains, ferromagnetic materials are usually multi-domain structures. The reasons why the domains in an unmagnetised sample are of a particular size lie beyond the scope of the present book.

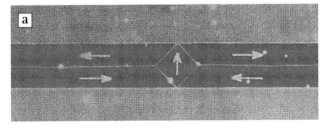

● **Figure 3.8** Domains in a single crystal of soft iron revealed by **a** Bitter's method and **b** the Kerr magneto-optic effect.

Magnetisation

When a material is magnetised, the domains are modified, so that one direction of magnetisation predominates, that of the external magnetic field. Using the domain model we can imagine two ways in which this could happen. In the first mechanism the domains change in size and shape. Under the influence of the external field, domains whose magnetisation is already in the direction of the field grow at the expense of other domains. As they grow, the domain walls move through the material. In the second mechanism the domain walls remain fixed while the atomic magnets swivel round to line up with the field. In fact both processes occur during magnetisation but the first happens more readily. Images, obtained by the techniques described in *box 3.2* show the first mechanism in action (*figure 3.9*).

Hard and soft magnetic materials

Permanent magnets are made from **hard magnetic materials** which do not readily lose their magnetism. Considerable energy is required to change or reverse its direction. We can combine our knowledge of microstructures from

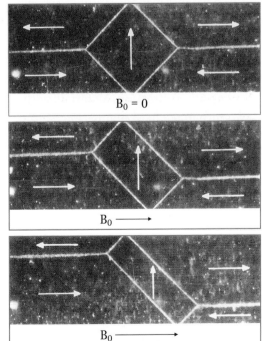

● **Figure 3.9** Photomicrographs of domains and domain motion in a single crystal of iron. The arrows show the direction of magnetisation of each domain. As the external magnetic field B_0 increases the favourably oriented domains grow.

chapter 1 with ideas from domain theory to predict factors which will make for a hard magnet.

It will be difficult to magnetise or remagnetise a material if the domain walls cannot move with ease; any feature which disrupts the regularity of the crystal structure will hinder their movement. We can therefore predict that the presence of grain boundaries, impurities and dislocations will tend to make a magnetic material 'hard'. In a **soft magnetic material** very little energy is expended in magnetising or reversing the magnetisation of a sample. Soft magnetic properties are associated with domain walls that move easily.

A magnetic material will also be hard if it is difficult to make the atomic dipoles rotate relative to the crystal structure. In a crystal of ferromagnetic material it is energetically favourable for the dipoles to line up parallel to certain crystallographic axes. As a result it is easier to magnetise the material along these axes. Some crystal structures have several favoured directions. Whatever the direction of the applied magnetic field, it is likely to lie close to one of these directions, making it relatively easy to magnetise the material. Materials with cubic crystal structures (chapter 1 page 9) tend to have soft magnetic properties for this reason. The opposite holds for materials with a hexagonal close-packed structure. The crystals are easy to magnetise along an axis at right angles to the close-packed planes, but much harder to magnetise in any other direction. Materials with the h.c.p. structure make hard magnets.

In general magnetic and mechanical softness do not go hand-in-hand. For instance, the 'soft' magnetic materials used in high-frequency transformers are often quite brittle.

SAQ 3.2

Use the domain theory and your knowledge of microstructures to suggest factors which are likely to produce a 'soft' magnetic material.

Saturation

The **saturation magnetism** is the maximum possible magnetisation that a material can achieve. It occurs when the magnetic dipoles in the domains are all aligned with the external magnetic field.

Magnetisation; the magnetic flux density B and the flux density causing magnetisation B_0

To go further we need to describe and quantify magnetic properties more precisely. We first look at the *cause* of a field. It is possible to calculate the magnetic flux density produced in a vacuum when a current flows through a straight wire or a coil. This quantity is the flux density causing magnetisation B_0. (The suffix signifies 'in vacuum'; in practice, air behaves like a vacuum.) B_0 depends *only* on the geometry of the coil and the size of the current. It can be varied by altering the current in the coil and, if the current is measured, the value of B_0 can be calculated.

The next step is to place a sample of ferromagnetic material in the magnetic field. You will have seen diagrams like *figure 3.10* before (*Physics 1*, *figure 15.5*). The lines of magnetic flux are drawn closer together as they pass through the sample. To describe this concentration of flux we say that the magnetic flux density, B, inside the material is greater than it was in the empty coil.

To measure B we look at its *effect* which could be a force or an induced potential. In practice the Hall probe (explained on page 41) is a convenient measuring instrument for this purpose.

The relationship between B and B_0 is not a simple one. It is best described by a graph. B_0, which can be varied by altering the current through the coil, is plotted along the x-axis. The measured value of B is plotted along the y-axis. The curve starts at the origin for an unmagnetised sample. The resulting curve as B_0 is increased,

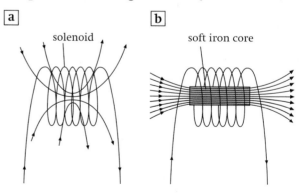

● **Figure 3.10**
a An empty air-filled coil; the lines of flux represent B_0.
b The same coil with a ferromagnetic core; the lines of flux are closer together. The magnetic flux density is B.

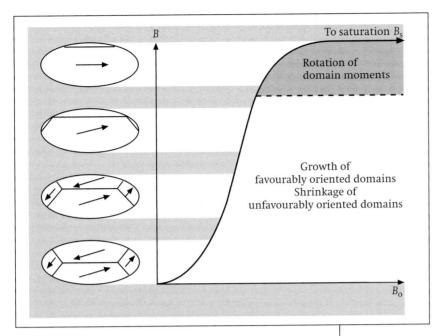

- **Figure 3.11** The magnetisation curve for a ferromagnetic material. The sample is unmagnetised at the start of the experiment. The insets show domain growth and rotation.

sometimes described as the initial magnetisation curve, is shown in *figure 3.11*. You can see that B increases to a limiting value. This is the saturation flux density B_S corresponding to the 'saturation magnetism' described above.

The inset sketches in *figure 3.11* explain what is going on at the domain level. At the origin the sample is unmagnetised and here the sketch shows the magnetism of the different domains combining to give zero magnetism. As B_0 increases the favourably oriented domains grow while the others shrink. During this stage B increases rapidly.

When the domain walls have moved as far as they can, dipole rotation comes into play. This only happens with difficulty. An increase in B_0 now produces a smaller change in B so that the curve flattens off. When the dipoles are aligned B reaches the saturation value, B_S, and the curve becomes horizontal.

Once the material has been magnetised to saturation, you might expect that removing the applied field (making $B_0 = 0$), would cause the material to become unmagnetised again, so that $B = 0$ also. However this is not the case. Removing the applied field leaves the material partially magnetised.

SAQ 3.3

What is the direction of B_0 in the domain pictures of *figure 3.11*? Imagine that the sample is again completely unmagnetised and that B_0 is increased from zero in the opposite direction. Sketch how the domains would change.

Magnetic hysteresis

In practical applications, of which the transformer is a prime example, materials often undergo a cycle of magnetisation and demagnetisation. The curve of B against the magnetising field, B_0, becomes a loop. It is called a **hysteresis loop** because B lags behind B_0 (hysteresis is the Greek word for 'lag'). The shape of the hysteresis loop is of paramount importance in engineering applications. Hysteresis loops can be observed using the equipment described in *box 3.3* on page 50.

Hysteresis loops

We now look at a hysteresis loop in more detail. The arrows in *figure 3.13* take us round it.

We start the cycle at A. Here the sample is fully magnetised in the direction of the external field. The value of B is the saturation flux density B_S. In the first stage of the cycle B_0 decreases. Be sure you follow the path shown by the arrow leading *from* A.

A → R The magnetic flux density in the sample decreases but when B_0 falls to zero the sample still retains some magnetisation. The intercept on the y-axis at R gives the flux density remaining in the sample.

R → C As the magnetising field B_0 passes through zero it reverses and starts to oppose the residual magnetisation in the sample. At C the magnetisation of the sample has been reduced to zero. The magnetisations of the different domains combine so that the sample has no net magnetisation.

C → D B_0 continues to increase in the reverse direction until the sample is saturated. B is again

Box 3.3 Observing hysteresis loops using an oscilloscope.

The use of a cathode ray oscilloscope (CRO) to determine the frequency of sound was described in *Physics 1*. The CRO was set up in the conventional way, which is to say, the scale on the *x*-axis measured time. Here, though, we need to make *x* represent B_0.

The circuit is set up as shown in *figure 3.12a*. The magnetising field, B_0, will be directly proportional to the current through the coil. The coil is in series with a potential divider (*Physics 1*). Here the circuit is being used to measure the current. The slide on the potential divider is adjusted to send a signal of suitable size to the CRO. Since this signal is directly proportional to the current it is also a measure of B_0. The CRO is set up so that the signal appears on the x-axis of the screen.

Meanwhile the voltage from the Hall probe goes on to the *y*-axis. We showed in chapter 2 that the Hall voltage is proportional to *B*.

The display on the screen (*figure 3.12b*) is a hysteresis loop. In the absence of a sample it would be a straight line through the origin.

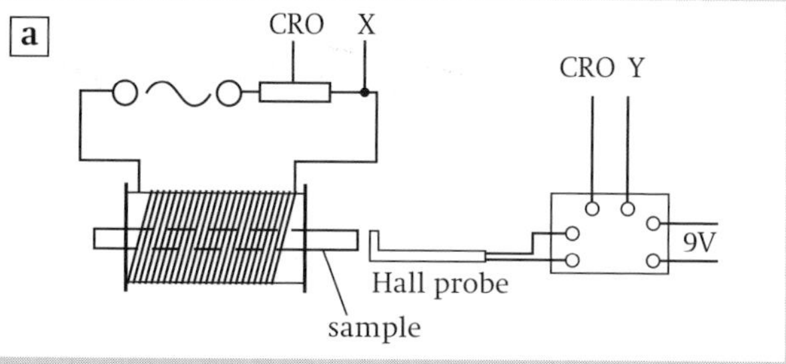

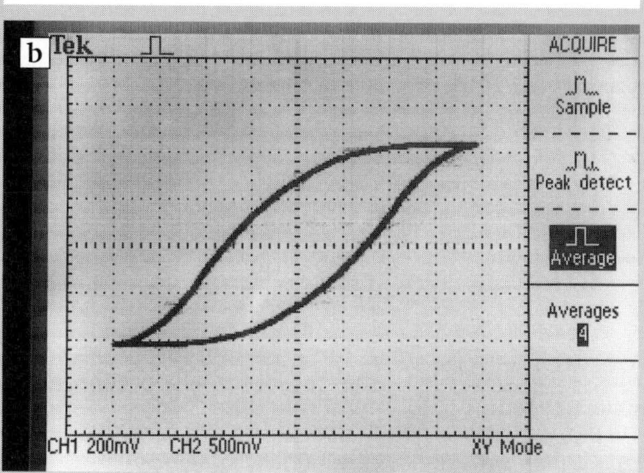

● **Figure 3.12**
a Circuit for demonstrating hysteresis loops.
b A typical hysteresis loop on the screen of a CRO.

equal to B_s but the sample is magnetised in the opposite direction.

D → Q In this stage of the cycle B_0 drops to zero and the flux density decreases to the value represented by the intercept on the *y*-axis. Notice that the loop is symmetrical, so that the flux densities at Q and R are equal and opposite.

Q → E B_0 now increases towards its original value. The sample becomes completely demagnetised at E. The magnetising field at E is equal and opposite to that at C.

E → A In the last stage of the loop the arrow leads back to A where the sample is once more fully magnetised in the original direction.

SAQ 3.4
Copy the hysteresis loop in *figure 3.13*. Add small sketches to show the magnetisation and domain walls at A,R,C,D,Q and E.

Interpreting hysteresis loops

The shape of the hysteresis loop characterises the magnetic properties of a material. In other books you may find the magnetising field at points C and E in *figure 3.13* called the 'coercive field'. It is the field needed to reduce the magnetic flux density in the sample to zero. There is no need for you to learn the term but you should recognise that this intercept is small in a 'soft' magnetic material. In a 'hard' magnetic material it will have a high value.

The value of the magnetic flux density at R and Q is called the 'remanence'. It represents the magnetic flux density left in the sample when the magnetising field is zero. Again you do not need to know the name for this intercept. You just need to remember that a high value characterises a

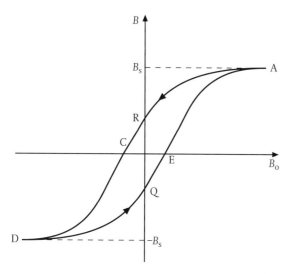

● **Figure 3.13** A typical hysteresis loop.

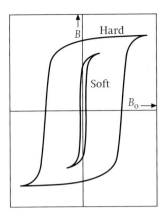

● **Figure 3.14** Typical hysteresis loops for 'hard' and 'soft' magnetic materials.

'hard' magnetic material and makes for a 'strong' permanent magnet. The hysteresis graphs in *figure 3.14* are typical of hard and soft magnetic materials.

SAQ 3.5

You have to select a magnetic material for the particles in the data-recording medium on a space-craft. The system must be able to withstand stray magnetic fields of up to 2×10^{-2} T; this is about 400 times higher than the magnetic field at the surface of the Earth. What feature will you look for in the hysteresis loop?

The area of the loop

The area enclosed by a hysteresis loop is proportional to the work done in going round it. It represents the energy dissipated in one cycle and is called the **hysteresis loss**. The 'lost' energy appears as internal energy (*Physics 2*, chapter 10).

You can see from *figure 3.14* that in a 'soft' magnetic material the curve has a small area and in a 'hard' magnetic material it has a large area.

Where does the energy go? We have seen that the domain walls move and atomic magnets rotate when a sample is magnetised. For the domain walls to move the atomic dipoles in the boundary layer have to twist. The magnetising field supplies the energy for this. It also provides the energy needed to rotate atomic dipoles within a domain; it is as if 'magnetic friction' makes it difficult for the dipoles to move past each other. Each cycle requires a new input of energy and this energy is eventually dissipated in heating up the material. Later you

will see how, in the selection of materials for transformer cores, an understanding of micro-structures helps to reduce the energy loss.

Curie temperature

One way to destroy permanent magnetism is to heat the magnet. At the atomic level, thermal energy keeps the electrons and atoms in a state of constant rapid motion. The movement becomes more vigorous as the temperature increases. It tends to shake structures apart and destroy any orderly patterns that exist. We saw earlier that the atomic dipoles in a magnetic material act in unison to produce a magnetic field. A coupling interaction keeps them aligned in a domain, but, as the temperature rises, thermal agitation disrupts the pattern and the magnetic flux density begins to decrease. It falls gradually at first and then more rapidly until, at a certain temperature, the interactions between the dipoles are completely swamped and the pattern is shaken to pieces. At this temperature, which is called the **Curie temperature**, the magnetic flux density drops to zero.

The graph in *figure 3.15* shows the effect of temperature on magnetisation for iron, cobalt and nickel. The saturation flux density, B_S, is plotted against the thermodynamic temperature. As the temperature increases, the magnetisation curve drops and cuts the axis at the Curie temperature (symbol T_C). Above this temperature the atoms are still magnetic but they behave independently, so that the magnetic effect is very weak. T_C is a characteristic property of a magnetic material.

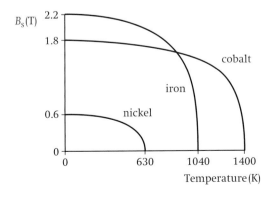

● **Figure 3.15** Temperature dependence of saturation magnetisation for Fe, Co and Ni.

Medium	$Co\gamma Fe_2O_3^{\dagger}$	CrO_2	$BaO(Fe_2O_3)_6$
Curie temperature (K)	860	390	590

$^{\dagger}Co\gamma Fe_2O_3$ is a particular magnetic form of Fe_2O_3.

● **Table 3.1** Possible media used for tapes and discs.

SAQ 3.6

The material used in the data–recording media on board a spacecraft must withstand operating temperatures of over 400 K. Use the values for T_C listed in *table 3.1* to select suitable materials.

SAQ 3.7

Suggest how hammering a permanent magnet can destroy its magnetism.

Energy losses in transformers

You met transformers in *Physics 2* (chapter 9) and will remember that they consist of two coils linked by a soft iron core. *Box 3.3* summarises the principles behind the operation of a transformer. Energy is transferred through the core by an oscillating magnetic field. The core provides an easy path for the magnetic flux. We now look at the efficiency of transformers and see which magnetic properties are the key to choosing suitable core materials.

Weight, volume and B_S

Transformers are heavy and expensive objects to buy and install. The amount of material in the core is largely responsible for their weight and cost. B_S, the saturation flux density, is significant because the core must have the capacity to carry all the magnetic flux needed to couple the primary and secondary coils. (Remember that the flux is oscillating, so that it has a certain 'peak' value.) In *Physics 2* the flux ϕ is defined as the flux density B multiplied by the perpendicular area A through which it flows. It is clear that the larger the value of B_S the smaller the cross-sectional area need be. It follows that a material with a high value of B_S will make a lighter and cheaper transformer.

Hysteresis losses, P_h

As mentioned earlier in the chapter, the area enclosed by a hysteresis loop represents the

Box 3.3 The transformer

Figure 3.16 is a schematic diagram of a transformer. An a.c. voltage V_1 applied across the primary coil causes a current, I_1, to flow round the coil. The alternating current produces an alternating magnetic flux which runs round the core in a 'magnetic circuit'. It cuts the secondary coil and induces a voltage V_2. If no flux is lost from the magnetic circuit the flux linking each turn of the first coil is the same as the flux linking each coil of the secondary coil. It follows that the e.m.f induced *per turn* of the secondary coil equals the e.m.f induced *per turn* in the primary coil.

For the coil we can write

$$\frac{\text{induced e.m.f. in primary}}{\text{induced e.m.f. in secondary}} = \frac{N_1}{N_2}$$

We now imagine an ideal situation in which the transformer is on 'open circuit' so that there is no load in the secondary circuit. No energy is being taken from the secondary coil. The induced e.m.f. in the primary coil exactly balances the applied e.m.f. so that no current flows in primary coil and no energy is taken from it. For this ideal transformer we can write

$$\frac{V_1}{V_2} = \frac{N_1}{N_2}$$

Transformers 'step up' or 'step down' voltages. Step-up transformers make it possible to transmit power at very high voltages over large distances between generators to consumers. The use of high voltages reduces the energy loss in the power lines. You saw how this loss can be calculated in *Physics 1* (chapter 11). At the consumer end step-down transformers reduce the voltage. Energy losses in the transformers themselves must be made as small as possible.

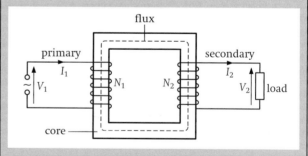

● **Figure 3.16** The basic features of a transformer.

energy lost in one cycle of magnetisation. The energy is dissipated as heat. It is highly desirable to make the hysteresis loss in a transformer core as low as possible. We therefore select a material with a hysteresis loop that is small in area.

The hysteresis power loss is given the symbol P_h. It will be proportional to the number of magnetising cycles per second and hence to the frequency at which the transformer operates. We can write this as:

$$P_h \propto f$$

There will be a hysteresis loss even when there is no load on the secondary coil (it is off-load). Because it occurs in the core it is sometimes known as a 'core loss' to distinguish it from the energy dissipated in the resistance of the coils when the transformer is on-load. In terms of domain theory, the core loss energy is used for moving domain walls and reorienting atomic magnets within the domains. You will see later how the microstructure of the core material can be made energy-efficient.

Eddy-current losses, P_e

In *Physics 2* you saw how a changing magnetic field can induce an e.m.f. The effect is not restricted to conductors in the form of wires. An e.m.f. can be induced in a bulk material causing currents to flow in loops inside the material. These are **eddy currents** and they are the source of eddy-current losses in transformer cores. Like hysteresis losses they are present when the transformer is off-load. They are greater if the core material is a good electrical conductor. The wasted energy causes the core to heat up.

To avoid this waste of energy, and the undesirable heating, measures are taken to keep eddy-current losses to a minimum. They include laminating the core by making it from thin sheets that are electrically insulated from each other. The magnetic flux lines are parallel to the sheet, each sheet carrying a fraction of the total flux. The reduced e.m.f. induced in a single sheet causes smaller currents to flow. To put it another

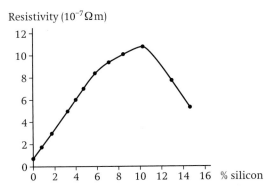

Resistivity $(10^{-7}\,\Omega\,\text{m})$

● **Figure 3.17** The effect of silicon concentration on the resistivity of iron.

way, the laminations break up the eddy-current flow.

Making the core from a material with a lower conductivity will also reduce eddy current losses. Alloys have higher resistivities than pure metals. Iron can be alloyed with a range of elements but silicon has the greatest effect in pushing up the resistivity. *Figure 3.17* shows how the resistivity varies with the percentage of silicon by mass. The cores of power transformers are commonly made from iron–silicon alloys. When mechanical properties are taken into account, the optimum composition turns out to be around 3% silicon.

Resistive power losses, P_R

When the transformer supplies energy to a load, currents flow in the primary and secondary coils. As a result power is lost in the coils. $P = I^2R$ is one of the three forms of the equation for electrical power.

Here it can be used to calculate P_R, the resistive power loss for the transformer. It is the loss in the primary coil added to that in the secondary coil so that

$$P_R = I_1^2 R_1 + I_2^2 R_2$$

Efficiency and energy losses

Energy losses reduce the *efficiency* of a transformer. In a device which transfers energy, the efficiency is the ratio of the output power to the input power. It is a fraction, which is sometimes expressed as a percentage.

$$\text{efficiency} = \frac{\text{output power}}{\text{input power}}$$

The output power combined with the power loss will equal the input power so that we can also write

$$\text{efficiency} = \frac{\text{output power}}{\text{output power + power loss}}$$

The power loss is made up of the resistive power losses in the windings, P_R, and the losses in the core, P_c. P_R only occurs if the transformer is on-load. P_c has two components: the hysteresis loss, P_h, and the eddy current loss, P_e. We can write

$$\text{power loss} = P_R + P_c = P_R + P_h + P_e$$

and

$$\text{efficiency} = \frac{\text{output power}}{\text{output power} + P_R + P_h + P_e}$$

Worked example

What is the efficiency of a transformer which delivers 5 kW of power to a load if the resistive power loss in the coils is 80 W and the core losses are 60 W?

Solution: Using the equation for efficiency we can write

$$\text{efficiency} = \frac{5000}{5000 + 80 + 60}$$
$$= \frac{5000}{5140}$$
$$= 0.97 \text{ or } 97\%$$

Energy-efficient microstructures

We have seen how an increase in resistivity can cut down eddy-current losses. We now look at the influence of microstructure on hysteresis losses. First, we take the energy used in changing the size and shape of the domains. Clearly the core needs to be made from a soft magnetic material, in which the domain walls can move freely. Ideally the material would be a single crystal, to eliminate grain boundaries. In fact the grains in a typical iron-silicon steel for a transformer coil are quite large (*figure 3.18*). The crystal structure also has to be as free of defects as possible. The material must be processed to remove dislocations as these impede the movement of domain walls. It also needs to be pure, as impurities introduce point defects which 'pin' the domain walls and prevent them from moving.

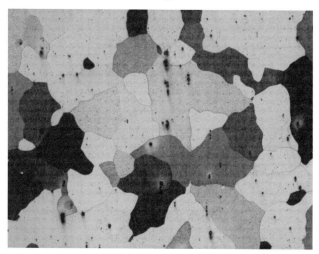

● **Figure 3.18** The grains in a silicon steel used for a transformer core. Each grain is about 0.5 cm across.

To be energy efficient a material must also be easy to magnetise in the direction of the applied field. We saw earlier that this holds for micro-structures where the dipoles can be readily oriented along several crystallographic directions. Iron-silicon, which has a cubic structure, behaves in this way. It can be made even more efficient if the grains are preferentially oriented during the production process. To achieve this the alloy is rolled and then **annealed** so that a direction of easy magnetisation lies parallel to the direction of the magnetic field in the transformer core. This is an example of a material where the microstructure is tailored for use in a very specific application.

SAQ 3.8

When a substance is annealed it is heated up and then allowed to cool slowly. Suggest why the oriented iron–silicon alloy used in transformer coils needs to be annealed after it has been rolled.

New materials for transformer cores

New developments include metallic glasses. They have amorphous microstructures and are made by very rapid solidification of the molten alloy (page 5). To achieve very rapid cooling the molten metal is delivered onto a rapidly rotating cooled drum (*figure 3.19*). As a result it forms as a thin ribbon. Amorphous materials are made from alloys of iron and boron with the addition of cobalt, silicon and neodymium. Because they are non-crystalline, all directions of magnetisation are equally favoured and the atomic magnets can

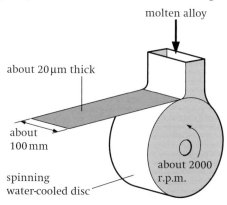

● **Figure 3.19** An amorphous metal is produced in the form of a ribbon. The molten alloy is delivered onto a spinning water-cooled drum for ultra-rapid cooling.

easily reorientate themselves in any direction. This makes it easy to achieve saturation. The domain walls can also move easily through the amorphous material.

An amorphous material has a further advantage in that amorphous structures have higher resistivities than crystalline ones. This, combined with the ribbon-like form, tends to reduce eddy current losses. Amorphous metals are used for the cores of small power transformers.

Efficiency and frequency

Both hysteresis and eddy current losses increase with the frequency. You can investigate how efficiency is affected in the following experiment.

An investigation to show how the efficiency of a transformer varies with frequency.

For this experiment a signal generator is used as a variable frequency power supply. The signal generator and the transformer should be selected so that they are compatible.

Connect up the circuit shown in *figure 3.20*. Two oscilloscopes monitor the voltage and current in the input and output circuits. The input power is V_1I_1 and the output power is V_2I_2.

Set the signal generator to give a sine wave of frequency 100 Hz. Adjust the signal generator voltage, V_1, to about 1.5 V amplitude or 3 V peak-to-peak. Measure V_2, the transformer output voltage and the currents I_1 and I_2.

Now use different values of f, the frequency, adjusting V_1 so that it remains at the same value.

Use the equation

$$\text{Efficiency} = \frac{\text{output power}}{\text{input power}} = \frac{V_2I_2}{V_1I_1}$$

to calculate the efficiency for each frequency. You can now plot a graph of efficiency against frequency.

The frequency dependence of eddy current losses

Faraday's law tells us that the magnitude of an induced e.m.f. is proportional to the rate of change of magnetic flux $d\Phi/dt$ (see *Physics 2*). Here we use it to explain how eddy current losses depend on frequency. At higher frequencies the rate of change of the flux is greater. You can predict, using Faraday's law, that the induced e.m.f.s and the size of the eddy currents will then increase. In fact it can be shown that eddy-current size is directly proportional to frequency. The power loss due to the eddy currents, P_e, will be directly proportional to I^2. Then, since $I \propto f$

$$P_e \propto f^2$$

Transformers have applications in the three frequency ranges shown in *table 3.2*. The core materials are selected for their performance at these frequencies.

Notice that an iron–nickel alloy is used in the cores of audiofrequency transformers. The reasons why it is preferred to iron–silicon are less to do with efficiency than with other requirements (sensitivity and fidelity) related to their use in communications equipment. We do not examine these in this book.

The equation for eddy-current power loss above predicts that the power loss increases with the square of the frequency. The loss would be very large in the high-frequency transformers used for

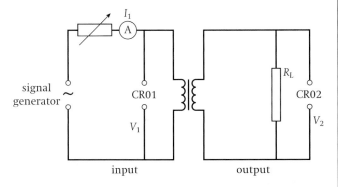

● **Figure 3.20** A signal generator feeds alternating current of different frequencies into a transformer. The two oscilloscopes monitor the voltage and current in the input and output circuits.

Transformer application	Material	Resistivity ρ ($\Omega\,\text{m}$)
Power 50 Hz	iron 3% silicon (oriented)	4.7×10^{-7}
	amorphous iron boron	1×10^{-3}
Audiofrequency	permalloy 45 (55% iron, 45% nickel)	4.5×10^{-7}
High-frequency	manganese zinc ferrites	0.1–2

● **Table 3.2** Soft magnetic materials for transformer cores.

signal processing unless a core material with a very high resistivity can be found. Soft ferrites, such as manganese-zinc ferrites are the answer. These materials were the results of a long-term research effort in the 1940s at Philips Research. Ferrites are **ferrimagnetic** materials (see *box 3.4*).

They are ceramics and have high resistivities. The resistivities of the types used in high-frequency transformers are between $0.1\,\Omega\,m$ and $2\,\Omega\,m$, but they can be made with much higher values for other applications.

Box 3.4 Ferrimagnetic materials

In this chapter we have discussed the ferromagnetism displayed by certain metals ('ferro-' meaning iron). Magnetite, the magnetic ore mentioned in the introduction at the beginning of the chapter, is an oxide of iron with the chemical composition Fe_3O_4. It belongs to a group of ceramic materials that are strongly magnetic. They are called ferrites and are described as ferrimagnetic although they do not necessarily contain iron. Their properties are typical of ceramics in that they have high electrical resistivities and are mechanically hard, brittle and chemically inert. In appearance they are dark grey or black. They are usually polycrystalline. Within the crystals there exist domains. When a ferrite is magnetised these domains behave in a similar way to those in a ferromagnetic material.

The domains arise from the spontaneous ordering of atomic magnets within the crystal lattice of the metal oxide but the ordering arrangement differs from that in a ferromagnetic material. In a ferrite crystal the atomic magnets lie on two interpenetrating sub-lattices. Within each sub-lattice the spins are all parallel but the spins in one sub-lattice are anti-parallel to the spins in the other. The two sub-lattices are not however magnetically equivalent. As a result the material has an overall magnetisation (*figure 3.21*).

Ferrites can be either soft or hard and both types are of great technical importance. Notice that 'soft' and 'hard' refer to magnetic and not to mechanical properties. Although the saturation magnetism of ferrimagnetic materials is lower than that of ferromagnetics, high electrical resistivity makes soft ferrites suitable for the cores of high-frequency transformers. The shape of their hysteresis curves makes hard ferrites very suitable for magnetic memory stores (e.g particles for discs).

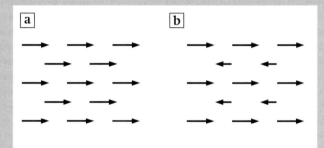

● **Figure 3.21** The ordering of the atomic magnets in **a** a ferromagnetic material, **b** a ferrimagnetic material.

SUMMARY

◆ Ferromagnetic solids are made up of small regions called domains. The atomic dipoles in each domain are aligned with each other.

◆ In a soft magnetic material (i) the domain walls can move easily and (ii) it is easy to rotate the dipoles within the domains. In a hard magnetic material the domain walls are not mobile and the atomic dipoles are realigned only with difficulty.

◆ When a material is fully magnetised it has reached saturation. All the magnetic dipoles are aligned with each other and with the external field.

◆ A graph of the magnetic flux density B against the flux density causing magnetisation B_0 for an initially unmagnetised specimen, has three regions. In the first stage B rises steeply as favourably oriented domains grow and others shrink. B then rises more slowly as the dipoles realign with the external field. As B reaches its saturation value B_S the curve becomes nearly horizontal.

◆ The B against B_0 graph is not reversible. When B_0 is reversed the graph goes on a different path and forms a closed loop, called the hysteresis loop. The shape of the hysteresis loop is characteristic of the material.

◆ Soft magnetic materials have a narrow hysteresis loop. Hard magnetic materials have a wide loop. The area of the hysteresis loop represents the energy dissipated in one cycle.

◆ If a ferromagnetic material is heated above its Curie temperature then the magnetic flux density falls to zero, because the alignment of the dipoles is completely disrupted.

◆ The power loss in a transformer core, P_C, is made up of the hysteresis losses P_h and the eddy current loss P_e. $P_C = P_h + P_e$

◆ If the transformer is on load there is also a resistive power loss, P_R.

◆ The efficiency of a transformer is given by the equation

$$\text{efficiency} = \frac{\text{output power}}{\text{input power}}$$

$$= \frac{\text{output power}}{\text{output power} + \text{power losses}}$$

where the power loss $= P_R + P_C = P_R + P_h + P_e$

◆ To improve the efficiency of a transformer the following factors must be considered:
  ● the saturation flux density should be high since the maximum flux is limited by this.
  ● hysteresis losses need to be kept to a minimum. To achieve this the material should allow domain walls to move freely and have several preferred directions of magnetisation.
  ● eddy currents should be kept low to reduce losses and prevent the heating of the core. High values of resistivity and a laminated structure cut down eddy-current losses.

◆ Materials with energy-efficient micro-structures have been developed for use in transformer cores. These include metallic glasses. Domain walls can move easily through amorphous structure; the atomic dipoles can easily reorient themselves and the higher resistivity reduces eddy-current losses.

Questions

1. Describe the domain structure in an unmagnetised sample of a ferromagnetic material.

2. A sample of a ferromagnetic material, initially unmagnetised, is placed in a increasing magnetic field. Sketch a graph to show how the flux density within the material increases. Use the domain theory to explain the changes that take place in the microstructure as the material is magnetised. Illustrate your answer with sketches showing the domains corresponding to different regions on the graph.

3. Sketch a hysteresis loop typical of a hard magnetic material. Using the same axes, sketch the hysteresis loop which would be obtained from a soft magnetic material for the same range of applied fields.

4. Iron has a Curie temperature of 770 °C. How will the magnetic properties of the iron differ above and below this temperature? Explain this change in properties in terms of the microstructure of the iron.

5. The loss in the core of a transformer P_C, is given by the equation

$$P_C = k_h f + k_e f^2$$

where $k_h f$ is the hysteresis loss and $k_e f^2$ is the eddy current loss.

   a. Use the information in the table to plot a graph of P_c / f against f.

f (Hz)	P_C (W)
40	88
60	180
80	300
100	460
120	650

   b. Use your graph to find the values of k_h and k_e.

   c. Calculate the hysteresis loss and the eddy current loss at a frequency of 50 Hz.

6. Metallic glasses have been developed for use in transformer cores. How does their microstructure make the core more energy-efficient?

CHAPTER 4

Optical properties of materials

By the end of this chapter you should be able to:

1. use *band theory* to describe why insulators absorb photons with a given range of energies but fail to absorb photons with energies below this range;

2. explain, in terms of their failure to absorb photons with the appropriate energies, why insulators can be transparent to visible light;

3. recall and use $E = hf$ to determine the energy condition for the transparency of an insulator;

4. use band theory to explain why metals are opaque to infra-red and visible light;

5. recall that the speed of electromagnetic radiation decreases as it passes from a medium of lower refractive index to a medium of higher refractive index;

6. appreciate that the transmission of light through glass may be limited by the presence of metallic impurities and their absorption of light;

7. recall that the microscopic density fluctuations in glass cause *Rayleigh scattering*;

8. recall that the amount of Rayleigh scattering is inversely proportional to the fourth power of the wavelength of the light scattered;

9. sketch and interpret graphical representations of the variation with wavelength of the percentage of visible and infra-red light transmitted per unit length of an optic fibre;

10. recall that the transmission of visible and infra-red light along optic fibres is affected by the absorption and scattering of photons;

11. recall that both laser and light-emitting diodes (LEDs) may be used to produce signals for transmission along optic fibres;

12. describe the advantages and disadvantages of lasers compared with LEDs for the transmission of signals along optic fibres;

13. describe how the *Planck constant* may be determined by making measurements of the minimum voltages needed to produce visible photons from LEDs of different colours.

Introduction

An 'optical property' is a response to visible light. (You might like to look back at *Physics 1*, chapters 16 to 18 to remind yourself about the properties of light and the models we use to explain them.) Here we will look particularly at the materials used in optical communication networks. The demand for systems which can handle more and more information has driven a new technology, photonics, where signals are made up of light photons instead of electrons. Light, because it has a high frequency, can carry enormous amount of information. Advances in optical communication have taken place in step with the development of new materials.

The fibres which transmit the light signals are made of ultra pure glass. The systems use optoelectronic devices based on semiconductors. These include the solid state lasers and light emitting diodes (LEDs) that convert electrical signals into light and the detectors that receive the signals. The need to make better components has stimulated the discovery of new classes of semiconductor materials.

At present optical fibres can transmit data at very high speeds but when the light reaches a switching point, such as a telephone exchange, the signal has to be converted to electricity before it can be re-routed to, say, a phone or modem. The electronic switches are relatively slow and create bottlenecks in the sytems. It is already possible to make purely 'photonic' devices, such as photonic transistors and optical logic gates, using new classes of semiconductor materials. These are much faster and may one day be used in communications. They could also be used in computers and some people foresee a time when optical computers will replace electronic machines.

The optical spectrum

Optical communication systems use wavelengths in the near infra-red part of the spectrum. We will therefore cover the interactions of materials with light in a wavelength range from about 0.4 μm to 20 μm. *Figure 4.1* will remind you that this is a very small region of the complete spectrum of electromagnetic radiation. The three scales in the diagram give wavelength, frequency and the energies of the corresponding photons. The frequency, f, and the wavelength, λ, are related to each other by the velocity of light, c. The equation is

$$c = f\lambda$$

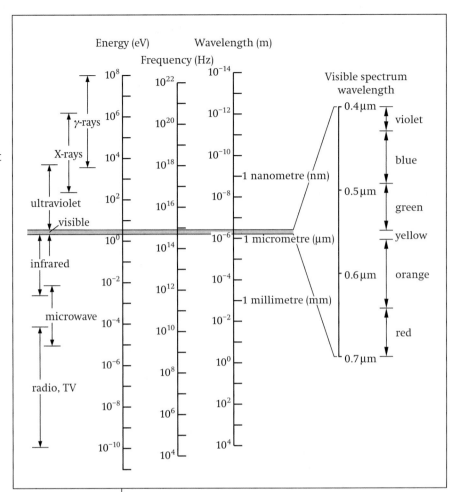

● **Figure 4.1** The spectrum of electromagnetic radiation, showing the wavelength range used in optical communication.

The energy, E, of the corresponding photon, is given by

$$E = hf \tag{1}$$

where h is the **Planck constant** (see *Physics 1*, chapter 16). The equations can be combined to give

$$E = \frac{hc}{\lambda} \tag{2}$$

SAQ 4.1

In 1999 the first blue–violet laser, with a wavelength of 405 nm, was made using the semiconductor gallium nitride. What is the frequency of this laser? How much energy does a single photon from this source have? The velocity of light is $3.00 \times 10^8 \, \text{m s}^{-1}$ and h, the Planck constant, is $6.63 \times 10^{-34} \, \text{J s}$.

The interaction of light with solid materials

When light energy travels from one medium into another several things may happen. The light can be reflected or transmitted by the interface and it can be absorbed by the medium it is entering. *Transparent* materials transmit light with relatively little reflection or absorption while those that absorb and reflect are described as *opaque*. Some materials are *translucent* which means that they transmit light but do not allow an observer to see through them. This happens because discontinuities inside the material 'scatter' the light so that it does not follow a straight path.

Metals have a lustrous appearance and are opaque to all visible wavelengths. Electrical insulators can be made to be transparent while semiconductors may be either transparent or opaque. You saw in chapter 2 how band theory can explain the electrical conductivity of solid materials. Here you will see how band structures account for the differences in the way metals and insulators interact with light.

How light interacts with atoms and electrons

We have two models for explaining the behaviour of light. In one light is made up of particles (photons) and in the other it is an electromagnetic wave. We cannot visualize, by making pictures in our imagination, how the two models can be equivalent. You saw in *Physics 1* that the wave model cannot account for the photoelectric effect. The particle model can explain it but not the so-

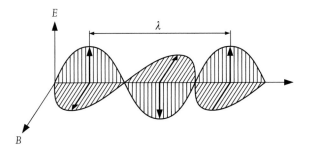

● **Figure 4.2** An electromagnetic wave showing the electric field E, the magnetic field B and the wavelength λ. The wave is travelling with a velocity c. E, B and c are at right angles to each other.

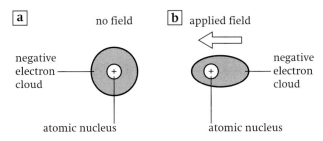

● **Figure 4.3**
a Schematic diagram of an atom considered as a positive charge surrounded by a negative electron cloud of uniform density.
b The same atom polarised by an electrical field. The negative electron cloud is displaced relative to the positive charge.

called 'wave properties' of interference and diffraction. Physicists have dealt with the dilemma by coining the phrase 'wave-particle duality'. Here you will see that we switch between the models as we need them.

Electronic polarisation

The diagram in *figure 4.2* shows light as an electromagnetic wave. One component is an oscillating electric field. The electron cloud surrounding an atom or molecule in the path of the wave may shift in response to the changing field (*figure 4.3*). This is called electronic polarisation and it can have two effects. The first is only important when the frequency of the light is close to a natural frequency of the electron cloud and is another example of resonance (see *Physics 2*, Chapter 4). At a resonant frequency the electron cloud vibrates and absorbs the energy of the radiation. The resonant frequencies for transparent solids lie in the ultraviolet region of the spectrum, outside the range used in optical communication.

The second effect of polarisation is an interaction which slows down the rate at which the light wave travels through the material. Energy is not absorbed. This change in the velocity of the light explains the phenomenon of refraction. The effect is important in optical fibres, where the refraction can be modified to improve transmission.

SAQ 4.2

Explain how the refraction of ripples on the surface of water can be demonstrated using a ripple tank.

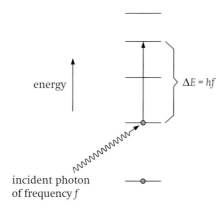

• **Figure 4.4** The energy levels in an isolated atom. An electron transition between two levels is shown. The energy of the photon is equal to the difference ΔE between the levels.

Electronic transitions

We now turn to the particle model and treat light as a stream of photons. *Figure 4.4* is a schematic diagram of the energy levels in an isolated atom. Electrons can only exist at these levels. Light energy can be absorbed if an electron accepts the energy of a photon and jumps the gap between the two levels. The jump is called an 'electron transition'. As you see from the diagram the electron can jump more than one level at a time. The energy difference between the levels, ΔE, must exactly equal the energy of the photon. We can write

$$\Delta E = hf$$

hf is the photon energy, f is the photon frequency and h is the Planck constant.

The electron absorbs all the energy of the photon. It does not stay at the higher level indefinitely but falls, usually very quickly, back to the lower level. As it falls back energy is released. Certain materials are able to re-emit visible light in a phenomenon called *luminescence* but this is unusual. In some materials impurities introduce levels within the energy gap so that the electron 'trickles' down in small steps. In other materials the energy is transferred into the vibrations and rotations of the atoms (internal energy).

What makes an insulator transparent?

What is it about the structure of an insulator that allows it to transmit light? The answer lies in its

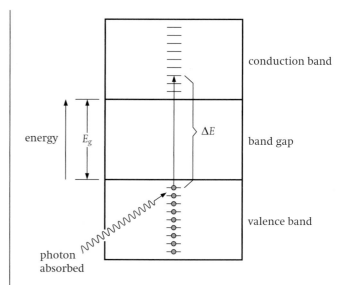

• **Figure 4.5** An electron accepts a photon of energy and jumps across the band gap. Note the empty levels in the conduction band and the full levels in the valence band.

band structure. You saw in chapter 2 that an insulator is only distinguished from a semi-conductor by the size of its band gap. In an insulator the gap is greater than 2 eV while in a semiconductor it is smaller.

For a material to be transparent photons of visible light must pass through it without being absorbed. If the material is an insulator the conduction band is empty. An electron in the valence band can accept the energy of a photon if this will enable it to make the jump up to the conduction band. Provided the energy of the photon is greater than the band gap E_g the transition is allowed. This is shown in *figure 4.5*.

We can now use the equation $E = hf$ to calculate what values the band gap in an insulator can have if it is to be transparent to light in the visible spectrum. We will look first at the long wavelength (low frequency) end of the spectrum.

The longest wavelength used in optical communication is in the near infrared at 1.55 μm. The corresponding photon energy can be calculated using equation (2)

$$E = \frac{hc}{\lambda}$$

h is equal to 6.63×10^{-34} J s and c is the velocity of light which is 3.00×10^8 m s^{-1}. One eV (electron-volt) is equivalent to 1.60×10^{-19} J. We can therefore write

$$E = \frac{6.63 \times 10^{-34} \times 3.00 \times 10^8}{1.55 \times 10^{-6} \times 1.60 \times 10^{-19}}$$

$$= 0.8 \, \text{eV}$$

An insulator with a band gap of 0.80 eV will absorb near infrared light of wavelength 1.55 μm and all the wavelengths shorter than this. It will be opaque to visible light. It will not absorb photons with energies smaller than 0.8 eV.

To transmit the wavelengths in visible light the band gap must be larger. You can see from *figure 4.1* that the wavelength in the visible part of the spectrum ranges from 0.4 μm to 0.7 μm. The photon energy corresponding to the shortest wavelength is

$$E = \frac{6.63 \times 10^{-34} \times 3.00 \times 10^8}{4.00 \times 10^{-7} \times 1.60 \times 10^{-19}}$$

$$= 3.1 \, \text{eV}$$

It follows that an insulator with a band gap of 3.1 eV will absorb wavelengths shorter than 0.4 μm but be transparent to the visible spectrum and longer wavelengths.

If the band gap is between 0.80 eV and 3.1 eV part of the visible light spectrum will be absorbed making the material appear coloured. This is illustrated in the following worked example.

Worked example

The energy gap in cadmium sulphide is 2.40 eV. What frequencies of visible light will it transmit and how does this explain its yellow-orange colour?

First we use equation (1) to calculate the frequency of a photon with an energy of 2.40 eV.

$$E = hf \qquad (1)$$

Remember that an eV (electron-volt) is equivalent to 1.60×10^{-19} J. h is equal to 6.63×10^{-34} J s so we can write

$$2.40 \times 1.60 \times 10^{-19} = 6.63 \times 10^{-34} f$$

Rearranging this equation gives

$$f = \frac{2.40 \times 1.60 \times 10^{-19}}{6.63 \times 10^{-34}}$$

$$= 5.8 \times 10^{14} \, \text{Hz}$$

You can find the corresponding wavelength by using $c = f\lambda$. c is the velocity of light, $3.00 \times 10^8 \, \text{m s}^{-1}$, so that

$$\lambda = \frac{3.00 \times 10^8}{5.8 \times 10^{14}}$$

$$= 0.52 \, \mu\text{m}$$

Cadmium sulphide will absorb all wavelengths shorter than this. You can see from the spectrum of visible light (*figure 4.1*) that this will cut out violet, blue and most green light. The result will be a yellow-orange colour.

SAQ 4.3
The energy gap of diamond is estimated to be 7 eV. What will be the highest frequency that the diamond can transmit? Where does this lie in the spectrum? Use h equal to 6.63×10^{-34} J s and remember that one eV (electron-volt) is equivalent to 1.60×10^{-19} J.

Why are metals opaque and shiny?
Figure 4.6 will remind you of the band structure of a metal. It shows the finely spaced energy levels in the conduction band. The band is partially full, with the free electrons occupying only the lower levels. Because the levels are extremely close

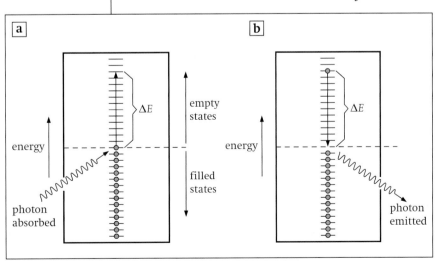

● **Figure 4.6** The conduction band in a metal, showing the finely spaced energy levels. In **a** an electron accepts a photon as it jumps into a higher unoccupied energy level. In **b** the photon is re-emitted by the transition of the electron to the lower energy state.

together the free electrons can accept photons with very low energies corresponding to the lowest frequencies in the electromagnetic spectrum. At higher frequencies the many unoccupied levels in the upper part of the band allow a continuous range of electronic transitions up to the ultraviolet. As a result metals are opaque to radio waves, microwaves, infrared and visible light. At the high frequency end of the spectrum (X- and γ-rays) they are transparent. Most metals become transparent in the middle of the ultraviolet range at a frequency which is a property of the metal.

The photons are absorbed by atoms in the outer surface of the metal. The light is completely absorbed by a very thin layer less than 0.1 μm thick. Most of the light is then re-emitted from the surface as photons of the same wavelength. *Figure 4.6b* shows the emission of a photon as an electron falls back to its original level in the band. Most metals reflect all the wavelengths in the visible spectrum by this mechanism. This gives them a silvery lustre. Although all metals show very strong general absorption, many also show selective absorption of certain wavelengths. Corresponding to this is the selective reflection of the same wavelengths. Thus copper has a red-orange colour. Gold appears yellow by reflected light for the same reason.

SAQ 4.4

The light transmitted by a very thin film of gold looks blue-green. Explain why.

Refractive index of fibre optic glass

The absolute refractive index (n) of a material is the ratio of the speed of light in free space to the speed of light in the material (see *Physics 1*, chapter 18). You saw earlier that light travels at a slower speed in a transparent medium because the electromagnetic wave interacts with the electron clouds surrounding each atom. If we want to describe the behaviour of light passing from one medium to another we can write

$$\frac{n_1}{n_2} = \frac{\text{speed of light in medium 2}}{\text{speed of light in medium 1}}$$

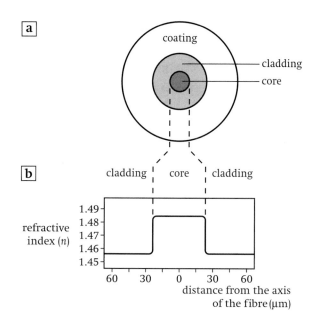

● **Figure 4.7**
a An optical fibre in cross-section showing the core, cladding and coating.
b Refractive index profile in a step-index fibre.

where n_1 is the refractive index of medium 1 and n_2 is the refractive index of medium 2. If the speed of the electromagnetic light decreases as it travels from medium 1 to medium 2 (i.e. speed of light in medium 1 > speed of light in medium 2) it follows that the refractive index of medium 1, n_1, is less than the refractive index of medium 2, n_2. If the speed increases, then the light is travelling from a medium of high refractive index to a medium of low refractive index. We will now see how understanding this relationship has solved a technological problem.

Figure 4.7a shows an optical fibre in cross-section. The outer layer is a protective coating. The core and the surrounding cladding are made of high purity silica glass modified by the controlled addition of very small amounts of other substances. Pure silica has a refractive index of 1.45 at 1 μm. Very small quantities of boron oxide (B_2O_3) can be added to lower the refractive index whilst the addition of compounds such as GeO_2 will cause it to increase. *Figure 4.7b* shows the refractive index profile. The refractive index changes sharply at the interface between the core and the cladding. Because of this, the fibre is known as a *step-index* fibre.

A problem which can arise in this type of fibre is illustrated in *figure 4.8*. Three rays of light are

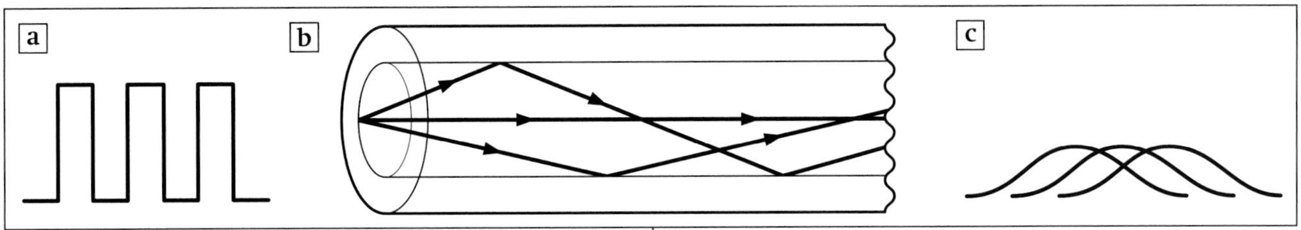

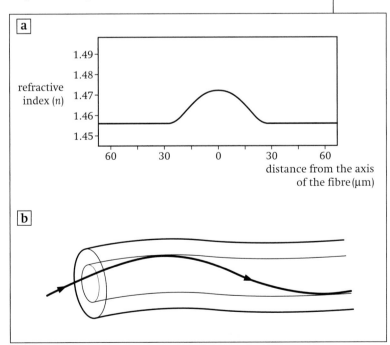

● **Figure 4.8** Three rays of light (**a**) take pathways of different length as they travel through a step-index optical fibre (**b**). As a result the optical pulses lose their sharp edges and the signal becomes blurred (**c**).

shown travelling along a length of optical fibre. The cladding keeps most of the light inside the fibre because total internal reflection occurs at the interface between the core and the cladding. A light ray can take many possible paths through the core and the cladding. The problem is that the pathway for a ray which travels down the centre is shorter than the pathway for light which travels at an angle to the axis of the length of the fibre. The signal is digital which means that it is made up of pulses of light. Each pulse lasts for a certain interval of time. If the pulses travel via pathways of different length they will arrive at a given point in the fibre at different times. The sharp edges of the pulses will be blurred and they will

become spread out over longer time intervals. If the fibre is long and if the pulses are close together they may overlap (you can see this happening in *figure 4.8*). It can become difficult to resolve the separate pulses when they reach the receiving end of the fibre. The effect is called modal or **multipath dispersion**.

One way of overcoming this problem is to make the diameter of the fibre very small. In effect only one beam, with a path down the centre of the core, is propagated. This type of fibre is described as *monomode*.

The other way is to tailor the refractive index of the fibre so that the light travels faster in the outer layers of the core than it does on the inside. *Figure 4.9a* shows the refractive index profile of this type of fibre, sometimes known as a **graded index fibre**. Notice that *n* is highest in the centre of the core. You know that a ray of light bends when it crosses an interface. Here the refractive index changes in a continuous fashion so that the ray follows a curving path (*figure 4.9b*). It eventually undergoes total internal reflection and curves back towards the centre of the fibre. The greater speed of the ray in the outer part of the core compensates for the longer path. There is no dispersion because zigzag rays take no more time to travel through a given length of fibre than rays passing straight down the centre of the core.

SAQ 4.5

The refractive index profile of a step-index fibre is shown in *figure 4.7b*. Take the values of the refractive index in the core and cladding and use them to calculate the critical angle *C*. You need to remember that

$$\frac{n_{\text{core}}}{n_{\text{cladding}}} = \frac{1}{\sin C}$$

● **Figure 4.9**
a The refractive index profile in a graded index fibre.
b The path of a ray travelling at an angle to the length of the fibre. The ray travels faster in the outer core where the refractive index is lower.

The transparency of fibre optic glass

Optical fibres used for communication have to be many kilometres long. Over such large distances any factor which reduces the intensity of the signal becomes important. In practical situations there is some loss of intensity because the fibres are distorted from an ideal straight line configuration. Here we are more concerned with processes that take place in the glass itself. Glass can absorb photons; it can also scatter them, so that they are deflected in many directions. You will see that the transparency of the glass used for optical fibres nowadays approaches the limits imposed by the atomic structure of the pure material.

Absorption of photons in glass

Fibre optic glass produced today is about 10 000 times more transparent than the purest glass available in the early 1960s. The dramatic improvement has been achieved mainly by eliminating impurities. Metallic ions such as copper, iron and vanadium absorb light in the visible and near infra-red spectrum. If you look at a pane of window glass through its side edges it appears green. The colour comes from metal ions dissolved in the glass. Electronic transitions in these ions absorb photons and by robbing the transmitted light of the corresponding wavelengths make it appear coloured. Very specialised methods have been developed for the manufacture of optical fibres and their use has reduced the concentrations of metal ions to a few parts per billion.

Hydroxyl ions are present as impurities in glass. They absorb in the near infrared and, although their concentrations have been reduced to very low levels, still account for significant reductions in intensity at certain wavelengths.

As the wavelength increases beyond $1.6\,\mu m$, the polar bonds between the atoms of the glass begin to vibrate in resonance with the wave frequencies. Infrared photons are absorbed to an increasing extent as the wavelength increases. Because it occurs even in the purest glass this process sets an upper limit on the wavelengths available for transmission.

Rayleigh scattering

When an electromagnetic wave passes through space it produces an oscillating electric field at each point in its path. If the space contains some electrons, attached to atoms or molecules, they are set into forced vibration by the field. The vibrating electrons then, in turn, radiate waves of their own. If the electrons are randomly spaced with an average spacing which is large compared with the wavelength of light they vibrate independently. The light is said to be scattered. Forced vibrations occur at frequencies below the resonant frequency (which is in the ultraviolet) so that scattering occurs in the visible and infrared spectrum. The effect is known as **Rayleigh scattering**. It is found that the intensity of the scattered light is proportional to $1/\lambda^4$. If λ_{red} is the wavelength of red light and λ_{blue} is the wavelength of red light we can write

$$\frac{\text{intensity of scattered blue light}}{\text{intensity of scattered red light}} = \frac{(\lambda_{red})^4}{(\lambda_{blue})^4}$$

If we take λ_{red} to be 700 nm and λ_{blue} to be 400nm then $(\lambda_{red})^4/(\lambda_{blue})^4$ will be $(7/4)^4$ i.e. 9.4. The blue light will therefore be scattered much more than the red (about 10 times as much). In the upper part of the atmosphere the molecules in the air are sufficiently far apart to produce scattering. If it were not for the atmosphere the sky would look perfectly black. The thickness of the atmosphere causes much of the light to reach the observer from directions making an angle with the direct line between sun and the observer, causing the sky to appear bright. Because blue light is scattered more than red it appears blue.

Scattering also explains the red or orange colour of the western sunset sky. Here the light passes through a greater thickness of the atmosphere and is also scattered by dust and mist particles in the lower part of the atmosphere. By the time it reaches us scattering has removed the blue light from the beam more efficiently than the red. As a result we see red and orange in the transmitted light.

Rayleigh scattering in glass

Rayleigh scattering occurs in glass and is important because it sets limits on the wavelength

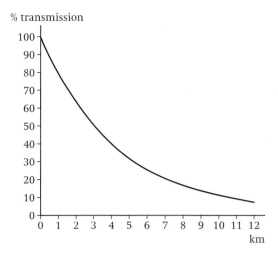

% transmission

● **Figure 4.10** Decrease in intensity of light as it is transmitted down an optic fibre. The percentage transmission per kilometre is 80%.

range in which optic fibres can transmit light. Glass has a disordered structure (chapter 1) which produces random fluctuations in its composition and density. The irregularities can act as centres for Rayleigh scattering. Again, the amount of scattering at a wavelength λ is inversely proportional to the fourth power of the wavelength. The reduction in intensity due to Rayleigh scattering is small at wavelengths in the near infrared but significant in the visible spectrum.

Choice of wavelength for transmission

To see how absorption and Rayleigh scattering reduce the amount of light transmitted by an optical fibre we can plot graphs with the wavelength of the light on the x-axis and the amount of light transmitted on the y-axis. There are several ways of quantifying the transmission. Here, we will use the percentage of light transmitted per kilometre, a unit which needs some explanation. Imagine a beam of light with intensity I_0 being launched into one end of a fibre and then travelling 1 km. If at this distance the intensity has been reduced to I_1 we can write

$$\text{transmission per kilometre} = \frac{I_1}{I_0} \times 100\%$$

As the signal travels on the same percentage will be lost in each kilometre of length. The graph in *figure 4.10* shows intensity transmitted against distance. In this example the transmission per

kilometre is 80% and the intensity of the signal entering the fibre is $1.0\,\text{MWm}^{-2}$. (This value corresponds to a signal with power 10 mW entering a fibre with diameter just over 0.1 mm.)

After 1 km the intensity will be reduced to $0.80\,\text{MW}\,\text{m}^{-2}$.

After 2 km the intensity will be reduced to 80% of $0.80\,\text{MW}\,\text{m}^{-2}$, i.e. $0.64\,\text{MW}\,\text{m}^{-2}$.

After 3 km the intensity will be reduced to 80% of $0.64\,\text{MW}\,\text{m}^{-2}$, i.e. $0.51\,\text{MW}\,\text{m}^{-2}$.

You will recognise the shape of the graph as similar to the exponential decay curve of a radio-active isotope. In the present case the exponential decay takes place over distance rather than time.

In *figure 4.11* the coarse dotted line shows the loss of intensity when the only mechanism causing a reduction in intensity is Rayleigh scattering of the photons. It is possible to show that, for this line,

$$\log_{10}\frac{I_1}{I_0} \propto \lambda^4$$

but we need not go into details of the calculation. You can see that the reduction in intensity becomes less important as the wavelength increases. At 1.55 µm Rayleigh scattering reduces the percentage of light transmitted by only 3%. However at this wavelength another process starts to come into play. This is the absorption of photons by the vibrating bonds in the lattice. It causes the percentage of light transmitted to fall steeply as the wavelength increases towards the infrared. The fine broken line shows what the transmitted intensity would be like if this were the only mechanism to cause a reduction. Photons are also absorbed by hydroxyl ion impurities; the thin solid line shows the transmission intensity if this were the only factor causing a reduction.

The thick solid line shows the percentage of light actually transmitted. All three reduction mechanisms can be seen in this curve.

SAQ 4.6 _____

Use the information in *figure 4.11* to suggest which wavelengths will be best for transmission through optical fibre. What region of the spectrum are they in?

The graph in *figure 4.11* shows that the percentage transmission is a maximum at about 1.55 μm, making this the preferred wavelength for a signal. This choice is based on the optical properties of the glass but there are other factors to consider. For instance, are emitters and detectors that operate at the selected wavelength available?

SAQ 4.7

The GaAlAs semiconductor laser was designed for optic fibre applications. It emits in the range 0.82 μm to 0.9 μm. Explain why, for optical communication purposes, this is not ideal.

● **Figure 4.12** A solid-state laser directs near-infrared light into an optic fibre.

Light sources (emitters)

The light sources, or emitters in optic fibre communication systems convert electrical signals into light at the transmitting end of the optic fibre. The photograph in *figure 4.12* shows a tiny infrared **laser** directing its output into a very thin glass fibre.

Emitters can be either light-emitting diodes (LEDs) or semiconductor lasers. In both light is emitted when the electrons and positive holes in a semiconductor material recombine. Each recombination produces a photon with an energy

that depends on the band gap energy in the semiconductor material. LEDs and lasers differ in the way they operate and in the character of the light they produce. *Box 4.1*, overleaf, explains in outline how they work.

We will now compare lasers and LEDs by seeing how well each type of emitter meets the requirements of optical communication systems. The points in favour of lasers are taken first, and the points where LEDs have the advantage follow. One of the most remarkable features of a laser is that

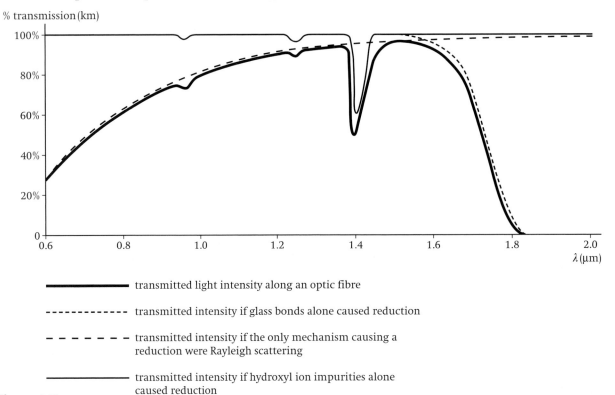

% transmission (km)

——————— transmitted light intensity along an optic fibre

- - - - - - - - - - - transmitted intensity if glass bonds alone caused reduction

— — — — — transmitted intensity if the only mechanism causing a reduction were Rayleigh scattering

——————— transmitted intensity if hydroxyl ion impurities alone caused reduction

● **Figure 4.11**

Box 4.1 How light emitting diodes and lasers work

The light emitting diode (LED)

Figure 4.13 shows the structure of an LED. At its heart there is a semiconductor chip which is shown schematically. Light comes out from the sides of an 'active layer'. This is the narrow zone between a layer of *p*-type material and a layer of *n*-type material. A voltage, applied at right angles to the layers, drives positive holes from the *p*-layer and electrons from the *n*-layer in opposite directions. They meet in the active layer where they recombine. Each recombination releases a photon of energy equal to the band gap in the active region. The photons escape from the sides of the active layer. The frequency of the photons determines the colour of the light. (LEDs are often housed in coloured lenses but you should note that these do not determine the colour of the light.)

A semiconductor laser

A semiconductor laser is built of many layers of varying composition and doping. *Figure 4.14a* is a cross-section through a GaInAsP/InP laser which emits infra-red light at a wavelength of 1.1–1.3 μm. The device is designed so that the electrons meet and recombine with the positive holes in the active region. In a laser this is the resonant cavity, the ends are essentially mirrors, so that the photon is confined in the region between them. The photons bounce back and forth inside the cavity, stimulating other electron pairs to recombine and emit more photons of the same wavelength. The photons are in phase with each other (see *Physics 1* chapter 19). They in turn stimulate more emissions so that the photon stream grows in intensity. One of the mirrors is semi-silvered so that when the photon stream builds up sufficient intensity it bursts through in a narrow beam of intense light (*figure 4.13b*). The light is coherent, meaning that all the oscillations are in phase with each other.

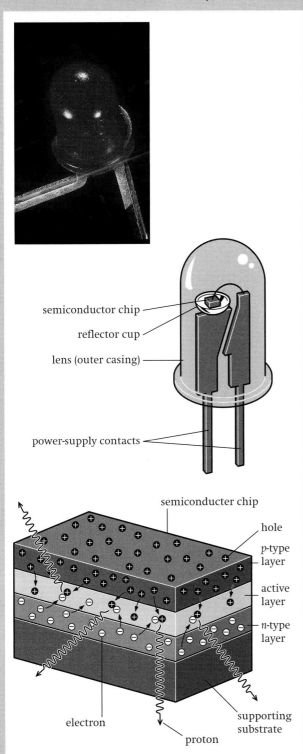

● **Figure 4.13** The structure of an LED.

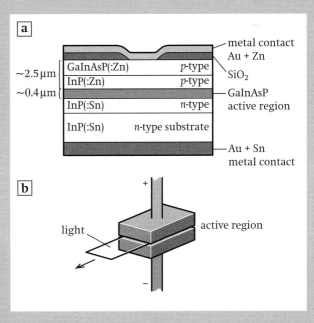

● **Figure 4.14**
a A cross section through a semiconductor laser. Note the small dimensions.
b The laser produces a narrow beam of intense light.

it produces coherent light. This is explained in *box 4.1* but you may like to note that it offers no advantage in this application.

Advantages of lasers

- The primary quality of a laser is its brightness. It radiates more power than an LED, the emitting area is smaller than in an LED and, as you see in *box 4.1*, the beam has parallel sides. The last property is called 'directionality' and is useful because it makes it easy to direct the beam into a fibre. The light from an LED does not behave like this; it spreads out in a diverging beam. The three factors combine to allow more power to enter an optical fibre from a laser than from an LED.

- Lasers switch very much faster than LEDs so that they can transmit more information in a given amount of time. They are also better suited to transmitting digital signals than LEDs. This is because in a laser very little radiation is emitted until the applied current reaches a threshold value when it rises very sharply. In an LED the intensity is more or less proportional to the applied current.

- Laser light has a narrower spread of frequencies than the light produced by an LED. This gives it an advantage in optical communication systems because it reduces undesirable effects due to dispersion.

Colour	Peak wavelength (μm)	Photon frequency, f (10^{14} Hz)
Red	0.635	4.72
Yellow	0.583	5.14
Green	0.565	5.30

- **Table 4.1**

When there is a spread of frequencies in the transmitted light dispersion occurs if the speed of light in the glass varies over the frequency range. It causes each frequency of light in the beam to reach the end of the fibre at a slightly different time, with the result that the signal becomes more difficult to resolve. This type of dispersion is known as **material dispersion** to distinguish it from multipath dispersion.

Advantages of LEDs

- The electronic circuits needed to drive LEDs are simpler than the circuits required for lasers.
- LEDs have longer lifetimes than lasers.
- LEDs are inexpensive compared with lasers. Emitter technology is advancing at a revolutionary pace. Both LEDs and lasers are constantly being improved. The lifetime of lasers is getting longer and the power of LEDs has increased. Apart from their use in communications LEDs may one day replace incandescent bulbs as a source of light power (*figure 4.15*).

The principle behind an LED was explained in *box 4.1*. Like the diode you met in *Physics 1* the LED has a characteristic voltage at which it will switch on and the current will begin to rise (*figure 4.16a*). When this happens in an LED you notice the first faint glow of light. This is the voltage needed to drive the electrons and positive holes into the active region and it is nearly equal to the energy gap voltage $\Delta E/e$ (volts). ΔE is a characteristic of the semiconducting material from which the diode is made. From the colour of the LED (or from the data supplied by the manufacturer) you can obtain the frequency of the light. This gives a very simple way of testing the relationship $\Delta E = hf$ and estimating a value for the Planck constant.

- **Figure 4.15** These modern LEDs, developed by Professor Colin Humphreys at Cambridge University, have now been made into full size traffic lights. They are much more robust than conventional bulbs, and they use far less electrical energy.

An experiment to determine a value of the Planck constant using LEDs of different colours

Set up the potential divider circuit shown in *figure 4.16b*. You can control the potential difference applied across the LED by sliding the jockey along the wire. You need to find the minimum voltage which will produce visible photons. It is a good idea to make a black cardboard tube, about 20 cm long and 4 cm diameter. You can look down this to observe the precise point when a very small movement of the jockey causes the LED *just* to glow. You can use a piece of dark cloth to prevent any background light from entering the bottom of the tube. Record the position of the jockey on the wire by measuring its position, *l*. Record the voltmeter reading V_0. If the length of the wire is *L*, you can calculate the value of the p.d. *V*, which *just* makes it glow. It will be

$$V = \frac{l}{L} V_0$$

Repeat with the other LEDs. The relationship between *V* and the frequency of the photons emitted by the LED is

$$eV = hf - C$$

h is the Planck constant and *C* is another constant. This relationship should give a graph like that in *figure 4.16c*.

If possible, look up the frequencies for the LEDs you have used. Typical manufacturers' data for red, green and yellow LEDs are given in *table 4.1*. Then plot a graph of *V* against *f*, and use it to find a value of the Planck constant.

a

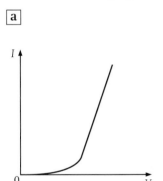

b

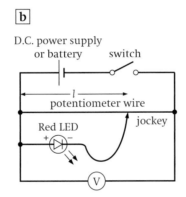

c

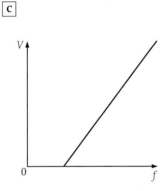

● **Figure 4.16**
a The current-voltage characteristic graph for an LED.
b Circuit for measuring the potential difference which just causes an LED to glow.
c Graph illustrating the relationship between the voltage at which an LED first starts to glow and the frequency *f* of the emitted photons.

SUMMARY

◆ If the energy gap in an insulator is ΔE then the insulator will absorb all photons with an energy $\geq \Delta E$. It will be transparent to all photons with an energy $< \Delta E$.

◆ The energy of a photon is related to its frequency by the equation

$E = hf$, where h is the Planck constant.

◆ If the energy gap in an insulator is ΔE it will absorb all photons of frequency $\geq \Delta E/h$. It will be transparent to all photons of frequency $< \Delta E/h$.

◆ Metals are opaque because they have partially full conduction bands. The band is made up of very finely spaced energy levels and because many levels are empty the metal can absorb even very low energy photons corresponding to the lowest frequencies in the electromagnetic spectrum. Metals are opaque to frequencies in the infrared and visible spectra and to lower frequencies.

◆ If n_1 is the refractive index of medium 1 and n_2 is the refractive index of medium 2 then

$$\frac{n_1}{n_2} = \frac{\text{speed of light in medium 2}}{\text{speed of light in medium 1}}$$

◆ This shows that when an electromagnetic radiation passes from a medium of low refractive index to a medium of higher refractive index (i.e. if $n_1 < n_2$) the speed of the wave will decrease.

◆ Metallic ions such as copper, iron and vanadium absorb light in the visible and near infrared spectrum. Optical fibre glass is manufactured by techniques that reduce the levels of these contaminants to such low levels that they no longer cause significant absorption.

◆ The disordered structure of glass produces random fluctuations in its composition and density. These irregularities can act as centres for Rayleigh scattering. The scattered photons bounce off in all directions.

◆ The intensity of the light scattered by Rayleigh scattering is inversely proportional to the fourth power of the wavelength of the light.

◆ A graph showing how the percentage of light transmitted per unit length of an optic fibre varies with wavelength shows that maximum transmission occurs at $1.55\,\mu\text{m}$ in the near infrared.

◆ As the wavelength decreases below the maximum value and gets closer to the visible range the loss of photons by Rayleigh scattering becomes important.

◆ As the wavelength increases beyond the maximum transmission value there is a steep reduction in intensity as photons are absorbed by resonating bonds in the glass.

◆ The advantages of lasers compared with LEDs when acting as emitters in optical communication systems include the following.
  ● Lasers allow more power to be coupled into an optic fibre because a laser radiates more power, has a smaller emitting area and is directional.
  ● Lasers switch faster than LEDs.
  ● Lasers transmit on a narrower range of frequencies than LEDs and therefore cause less dispersion.

◆ The advantages of LEDs over lasers include the following.
  ● LEDs require simpler circuits than lasers.
  ● LEDs have longer lifetimes.
  ● LEDs are cheaper.

Questions

1 Explain, in terms of band theory, why insulators can be transparent to visible light.

2 Zinc telluride has a band gap of 2.26 eV. Over what range of wavelengths in the visible spectrum will it be transparent?

3 Use band theory to explain why metals are opaque to visible light.

4 a The transmission of signals over long distances along an optic fibre is possible because the glass is of very high purity. Describe two processes which reduce the intensity of a transmitted signal in pure silica glass.

b Sketch a graph to show how the transmission of light through an optic fibre varies with wavelength. Indicate, on your graph, the process chiefly responsible for the reduction in intensity in the different regions of the wavelength range.

c High-capacity telephone links operate at wavelengths in the range 1.3 μm to 1.55 μm. Suggest reasons for this choice.

5 Give three advantages and three disadvantages of lasers compared with LEDs for the generation of signals to be transmitted along optic fibres.

Answers to self-assessment questions

Chapter 1

1.1 **a** Spectacle lenses: using polymers it is possible to make lighter thinner lenses.

  Bottles for fizzy drinks: polymers make safer, lighter bottles. PET bottles are 25% more energy efficient to make than glass bottles.

b Advantages of glass are higher softening point, highly resistant to corrosion and environmental degradation (plastics are attacked by UV, strong detergents etc.)

1.2 X-ray diffraction, electron diffraction and neutron diffraction can be used to determine the arrangement and spacings of atoms in a solid. X-rays, electrons and neutrons all have wavelengths similar to atomic spacings, permitting diffraction measurements to be made.

  Neutrons interact with the nucleus of an atom whereas X-rays and electrons interact with the electron cloud. This means that the diffraction of neutrons is not strongly related to atomic number, unlike X-rays and electrons where the interaction depends on the number of electrons surrounding the nucleus and hence on the atomic number. This enables neutrons to sense the positions of light atoms, such as hydrogen, in the presence of heavier ones. As a result neutron diffraction is particularly useful for the study of hydrogen-rich compounds.

1.3 The volume of the sample of iron will decrease as the crystal structure changes from b.c.c. to f.c.c. The contraction occurs because f.c.c. is a close-packed structure while b.c.c. is not. As a result the volume of a f.c.c. crystal structure is smaller than that of a b.c.c. crystal structure containing the same number of atoms.

1.4 You can see that most of the fruit stacks are pyramids, several with flat tops. The sloping surfaces of the pyramids are close-packed. They correspond to the four 'families' of close-packed planes of the f.c.c. structure (the relationship of the close-packed planes to the cubic crystal was illustrated in figures 1.13 and 1.14). Thus the packing in the display is face-centred cubic (f.c.c.).

1.5 3.0×10^{-10} m

1.6 Stress = load/cross-sectional area. Stress (symbol σ) is the load applied to a specimen divided by its cross-sectional area before any deformation. Stress defined in this way is sometimes known as engineering stress.

  Strain = extension/original length. Strain (symbol ε) is the extension per unit length produced by tensile or compressive forces.

  The units of stress are Pa or Nm^{-2}.

  Strain is often expressed as a percentage.

1.7 A will have the higher value of the Young modulus since the force separation curve is steeper at the equilibrium separation.

1.8 The photomicrograph suggests that the crystal structure of copper is f.c.c. The evidence is the two sets of parallel yet intersecting lines which can be seen on most of the grains. They are the slip lines. The presence of families of slip lines in more than one direction in a single grain is an indication that the close-packing is f.c.c. rather than h.c.p.

1.9 The extension produced when one dislocation moves right through a crystal will be about 10^{-10} m. It will therefore take $10^{-3}/10^{-10}$ i.e. 10^{7} dislocations to produce a permanent extension of 1 mm. *Note*: A sample of metal or alloy used in engineering will have more than 10^{5} km of dislocations in a cubic centimetre.

Chapter 2

2.1 conductivity, $\sigma = \dfrac{1}{\text{resistivity, } \rho}$

The conductivity of silver is therefore

$\dfrac{1}{1.60} \times 10^{-8}$ or $6.25 \times 10^7 \, \Omega^{-1} \, m^{-1}$.

2.2 **a** The direction of an electric field represents the direction of the force it would exert on a positive charge. Since electrons are negatively charged the force exerted by the field is in the opposite direction.

b We are concerned with the rate at which the electrons are moving in a particular direction, that in which the electric current flows.

2.3 $t = \dfrac{1}{v} = 6.80 \times 10^3 \, s = 113$ minutes.

2.4 Flicking the light switch establishes an electric field at the speed at which an electric pulse can travel along a wire. This speed is between 2 and $3 \times 10^8 \, m \, s^{-1}$, almost a million million times greater than the drift velocity of the electrons. All the electrons drift under the influence of the field so that a flow of charge is set up almost instantaneously all along the wire.

2.5 The wavelength of the emitted radiation depends on the amount of energy released when an excited electron falls back to a lower energy level. When the atoms are close together in a solid they have energy bands made up of very closely spaced energy levels so that the electrons can make downward energy jumps of all sizes within a certain range. This produces radiation with corresponding wavelengths so forming a continuous spectrum in this range.

In the vapour phase the electrons can only occupy the relatively few energy levels belonging to the isolated atoms. Whenever the electrons release energy by moving between a particular pair of levels exactly the same amount of energy is released in each atom. The wavelength of the emitted radiation has a correspondingly exact value and produces a sharp line in the spectrum.

2.6 The current is made up of two components: a flow of free electrons in one direction and a flow of positive holes in the opposite direction. Although electrons and positive holes carry charges of equal magnitude the electrons are more mobile, travelling about three times faster than the positive holes. So in pure silicon, where the number densities are equal, the electrons contribute about 75% of the current.

2.7 In an intrinsic semiconductor there is one positive hole in the valence band for every free electron in the conduction band. The number density of electrons must therefore be equal to the number density of positive holes.

2.8 R varies most rapidly in the temperature range from room temperature to $50\,^{\circ}C$. Over this range the sensitivity of a sensor using a thermistor of this type would therefore be high making it a useful temperature probe.

2.9 **a** An increase in temperature increases the probability that an electron can gain enough energy to escape from the valence band into the conduction band. At normal temperatures diamond is an insulator because none of the electrons in the valence band have enough energy to jump across the large energy gap of $5\,eV$. At very high temperatures a few electrons have enough energy to escape so that the diamond becomes an electrical conductor.

b At room temperature just a few electrons in the valence band of silicon have enough energy to jump across the energy gap into the conduction band. In very cold silicon no electrons have sufficient thermal energy to escape; the valence band is completely full and there are no free electrons in the conductance band.

2.10 The relationship between the drift velocity v and the current I flowing in a conductor of cross-sectional area A is $I = nAve$ where n is the number density of the electrons and e is the charge on an electron. This equation can be rearranged to give $v = I/nAe$. If the current and the cross-sectional area are kept constant the drift velocity in a sample will be inversely proportional to the number density of the electrons. Since the number density of the electrons in a metal is very much greater than the number density of the charge carriers in a semiconductor the drift velocity in the semiconductor will be very much higher.

The equation $V_H = Bvd$ shows that the Hall voltage V_H is directly proportional to the drift velocity v provided that B and d have the same values. V_H will therefore be very much larger in a semiconductor than in a metal.

2.11 **a** $V_H = Bvd$

$= 2.2 \times 3.8 \times 10^{-4} \times 5.0 \times 10^{-3}$

$= 4.2 \times 10^{-6}\,\text{V}$ or $4.2\,\mu\text{V}$

b Hall voltages in metals were too small to be readily measured. The effect only found applications with the advent of pure semi-conducting materials in the second half of the 20th century.

Chapter 3

3.1

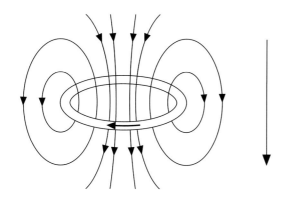

● **Answer** to SAQ 3.1

3.2 The ideal 'soft' magnetic material would have no grain boundaries and would therefore be a single crystal. It would be pure and have no structural defects such as dislocations. It would have a crystal structure that would make it easy for the atomic magnets to reorient themselves in the direction of the field.

3.3 In *figure 3.11* B_0 acts in a direction from left to right in the plane of the page.

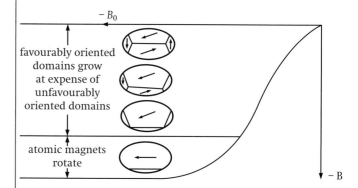

● **Answer** to SAQ 3.3

3.4

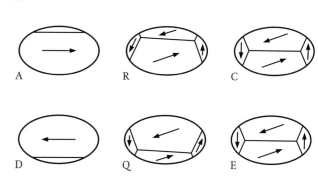

● **Answer** to SAQ 3.4

3.5 The magnetic material needs to be hard so that once magnetised it will retain its magnetism in the presence of stray magnetic fields. The shape of the hysteresis curve will therefore be similar to that for the hard material in *figure 3.14*. The value of the intercept on the B_0 axis (the field needed to reduce the magnetic flux density in the sample to zero) must be greater than 2×10^{-2} T. The value must not, however, be too high as the particles would then be too difficult to magnetise.

3.6 The particles in the recording media will lose their magnetism at the Curie temperature, T_C. CrO_2 has a T_C value below the limit and should therefore be rejected. The other materials are all right.

3.7 Hammering a permanent magnet will shake the microstructure allowing domain walls to move and atomic dipoles to become reoriented. If there is no external magnetic field the resulting material will have zero net magnetisation.

3.8 Rolling introduces dislocations which hinder the movement of domain walls, making the magnet harder and increasing hysteresis losses. Annealing frees the dislocations which move to the edges of the grains. In this way the process of annealing minimises hysteresis losses.

Chapter 4

4.1 The frequency of the laser can be found using the equation $c = f\lambda$.
$f = v/\lambda = 3.00 \times 10^8/405 \times 10^{-9} = 7.41 \times 10^{14}$ Hz
The energy of a single photon from this source is given by $E = hf$.
$E = 6.63 \times 10^{-34} \times 7.41 \times 10^{14}$
$= 4.91 \times 10^{-19}$ J (3.07 eV)

4.2 The speed of ripples on the surface of shallow water depends on the depth of the water. If a glass plate is submerged in the tank the ripples will travel more slowly in the shallower water above the plate. Where they cross the step formed by the edge of the plate the effect of refraction may be seen as a change in the direction of the waves.

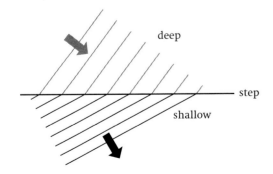

● **Answer** to SAQ 4.2

4.3 The band gap is 7 eV or 1.12×10^{-18} J. The frequency of a photon with this energy can be found using the equation $E = hf$.
$f = E/h = 1.12 \times 10^{-18}/6.63 \times 10^{-34}$ i.e. 1.69×10^{15} Hz
The highest frequency that the diamond will transmit will be just below 1.69×10^{15} Hz in the ultraviolet region of the spectrum. Radiation of this and higher frequencies will be absorbed.

4.4 Gold appears yellow in reflected light because the yellow wavelengths are selectively absorbed by a very thin layer on the surface and then re-emitted as photons of the same wavelength. A very thin film transmits light of a blue-green colour because the transmitted light has been robbed of yellow wavelengths.

4.5 $\sin C = n_{cladding}/n_{core} = 1.456/1.485 = 0.9805$
$C = \sin^{-1} 0.9805 = 78.7°$

4.6 1.45 to 1.65 μm, also around 1.3 μm. These wavelengths are in the infra-red region of the spectrum.

4.7 Earlier fibres transmitted light most efficiently at wavelengths from 0.82 μm to 0.9 μm so that the GaAlAs laser was an ideal emitter. As fibres improved the wavelengths for minimum transmission loss shifted towards the infra-red, to a wavelength nearer to 1.5 μm. The GaAlAs laser is not suitable for wavelengths in this range (the InGaAsP laser is the preferred source).

Glossary

amorphous a non-crystalline solid is described as amorphous. The structure of an amorphous solid is disordered. Glass, rubber and some polymers are examples.

alloy a metallic substance which is made up of two or more elements.

atomic force microscopy/scanning tunnelling microscopy a technique which images atomic positions by measuring the force exerted on a fine needle traversed across the sample. The micrograph is a computer visualisation of the surface.

band theory a theory which explains many properties of solid materials. Electrons can have energies within one or more broad bands. The bands may overlap or there may be a forbidden gap between them (see **energy gap**).

ceramic ceramics are inorganic compounds of metallic and non-metallic elements. They are crystalline solids produced by the action of heat on crystals of single or mixtures of inorganic non-metallic substances. Ceramics include pottery and stone, concrete and other materials used in the construction industry. Glass is not a true ceramic although it shares many similar properties.

close-packed in a close-packed crystal or plane the atoms are thought of as hard spheres that are packed together as closely as geometry will allow.

composite a material made up from one or more different classes of material (metals, polymers, ceramics and glasses). Composites are designed to combine the best characteristics of their component materials.

conduction band in solid materials this is an empty or partially empty electron energy band. It is made up of very closely spaced energy levels. Electrons in the band conduct electricity because they can be excited to higher levels within it.

conductivity, electrical, σ the reciprocal of the resistivity ρ. Defined by the equation $\sigma = l/RA$, where R is the resistance of a sample of cross-sectional area A and length l. Electrical conductivity is the reciprocal of resistivity.

crystalline in the crystalline state atoms or ions are arranged in a regular repeating pattern which extends in three dimensions over distances which are very large in comparison with interatomic distances.

Curie temperature the temperature above which a ferromagnetic material loses its ferromagnetism. At higher temperatures the alignment of neighbouring atomic magnets is disrupted.

dislocation a linear defect in a crystal which moves in response to an applied stress to produce plastic deformation. The line represents a misalignment of the atoms or ions in a crystal. A dislocation occurs when an extra half plane of atoms is present.

dispersion in optical fibres dispersion is a phenomenon which causes different rays in the same light pulse to take different times to travel down the same length of fibre. **Multipath dispersion** occurs when the rays have different path lengths in the fibre. **Material dispersion** occurs because rays with different wavelengths travel at different speeds.

domain a region of a ferromagnetic or ferrimagnetic material in which all the atomic magnets are aligned in the same direction. A domain is three-dimensional.

doping the controlled introduction of very small amounts of impurity atoms into a semiconductor material. Doping is used to modify the energy band gap in a semiconductor.

drift velocity the average resultant velocity of the charge carriers in the direction of the current flowing in a metal or semiconductor.

eddy current an electric current induced in a block of conducting material by a change in magnetic flux.

elastic deformation when an object recovers its original dimensions after an applied load is removed the deformation is said to be elastic. Above a certain limiting stress, the **elastic limit**, some of the strain becomes permanent (plastic deformation).

energy gap for intrinsic semiconductors and insulators there is an energy gap between the valence and conduction bands. Electrons are forbidden to have energies which lie in the gap.

equilibrium separation each atom in a solid vibrates about a central position. The equilibrium separation is the distance between the centres for two neighbouring atoms in a stable structure. In terms of the force-separation curve for two atoms it is the separation when the resultant force between the atoms is zero.

ferrimagnetic materials ceramic materials which can be strongly magnetised. The large magnetisations may be permanent or temporary.

ferromagnetic materials metals (e.g. Fe, Ni, Co) which can be strongly magnetised. The large magnetisations may be permanent or temporary. They result from the parallel alignment of atomic magnets in domains.

glass glasses are non-crystalline materials, often based on silica. They are not true ceramics although they have many similar properties.

glassy polymer an amorphous polymer. Glassy polymers share some properties with glass. They differ from semicrystalline polymers which are partially crystalline.

grain an individual crystal in a polycrystalline solid. The crystal structure inside a single grain is continuous. The interface between two grains is called a **grain boundary**. The crystal lattice has a different orientation on either side of the boundary.

Hall effect a magnetic field applied at right angles to a sample of metal or semiconductor along which a current is flowing causes a lateral displacement of charge. A potential difference can be measured if a voltmeter is connected across the sample in a direction perpendicular to both the current and the magnetic field. This is the Hall effect. The sign of the potential difference gives the sign of the majority charge carriers in the sample.

Hall voltage V_H the voltage produced by the Hall effect. A **Hall probe** is a thin slice of semiconducting material across which a Hall Voltage is produced when there is a magnetic field at right angles to the probe. It is used to measure magnetic flux density.

hard magnetic material ferromagnetic or ferrimagnetic materials used to make permanent magnets. They retain their magnetisation after the magnetising field is removed and are difficult to demagnetise.

hysteresis (magnetic) the lack of reversibility in the process by which a ferromagnetic or ferrimagnetic material is magnetised by an external magnetic field. The magnetic flux density B in the sample lags behind the magnetising field B_0.

hysteresis loop the closed curve produced when a sample of magnetic material undergoes a cycle of magnetisation and demagnetisation. Hard magnetic materials have wide hysteresis loops. Soft magnetic materials have narrow hysteresis loops.

hysteresis loss the energy lost in one cycle of magnetisation and demagnetisation. It is proportional to the area enclosed by the hysteresis loop.

intrinsic semiconductor a pure (undoped) semiconductor material in which the electrical conductivity depends only on the temperature and the band energy gap for that material.

laser acronym for Light Amplification by Stimulated Emission of Radiation. Semiconductor lasers give high intensity, easily directed light signals suitable for optical communication networks.

lattice the network of points on which a crystal structure is based.

material dispersion *see* **dispersion**.

multipath dispersion *see* **dispersion**.

number density the number of charge carriers (electrons or positive holes) present in unit volume of a metal or semiconductor.

Planck's constant h a universal constant that has a value of 6.63×10^{-34} J s. The energy of a photon of electromagnetic radiation E is related to the radiation frequency f by the equation $E = hf$ where h is the Planck constant.

plastic deformation permanent deformation which is not recovered when the applied load is removed. The atoms in the material are permanently displaced.

point defect a defect in a crystal associated with an individual atomic site.

polycrystalline material a material made up of many crystals or grains.

root mean square (r.m.s.) speed the r.m.s. speed may be calculated for molecules in a gas or free electrons in a metal. In metals free electrons have r.m.s. speeds of up to 10^6 m s^{-1}.

Rayleigh scattering the scattering of light by very small particles. It is responsible for unavoidable transmission losses in optic fibres where irregularities in the glass act as scattering centres.

saturation magnetism the maximum magnetisation (or magnetic flux density B_S) for a ferromagnetic or ferrimagnetic material.

semi-crystalline polymer a polymer in which some regions are amorphous and others crystalline. In the amorphous regions the molecules are disordered but in the crystalline regions they are aligned.

slip plane a crystallographic plane along which slip (the movement of a dislocation) can occur. Slip planes are usually close-packed.

soft magnetic material a ferromagnetic or ferrimagnetic material which may be magnetised and demagnetised with ease.

superconductor a material that conducts with no appreciable resistance at temperatures approaching absolute zero. The so-called **high-temperature superconductors** have this property at the temperature of liquid nitrogen (77 K).

tough a term used to describe a material which is resistant to fracture. **Toughness** is a measure of the amount of energy absorbed by a material as it fractures.

transition temperature the temperature at which the electrical resistance of a superconducting material suddenly drops to zero. Below this temperature the material conducts with no appreciable resistance. This temperature is also referred to as the critical temperature.

ultimate tensile strength (also known as **tensile strength**) the maximum value of the stress, in tension, that can be sustained before a solid breaks apart.

unit cell the basic arrangement of atoms which repeats to form a crystal.

vacancy an empty site in a crystal lattice from which an atom or ion is missing.

valence band in solid materials this is the electron energy band which contains the valence electrons.

Young modulus the ratio of tensile stress to tensile strain in a material that obeys Hooke's law.

Index